The *MYSTERY FANcier*

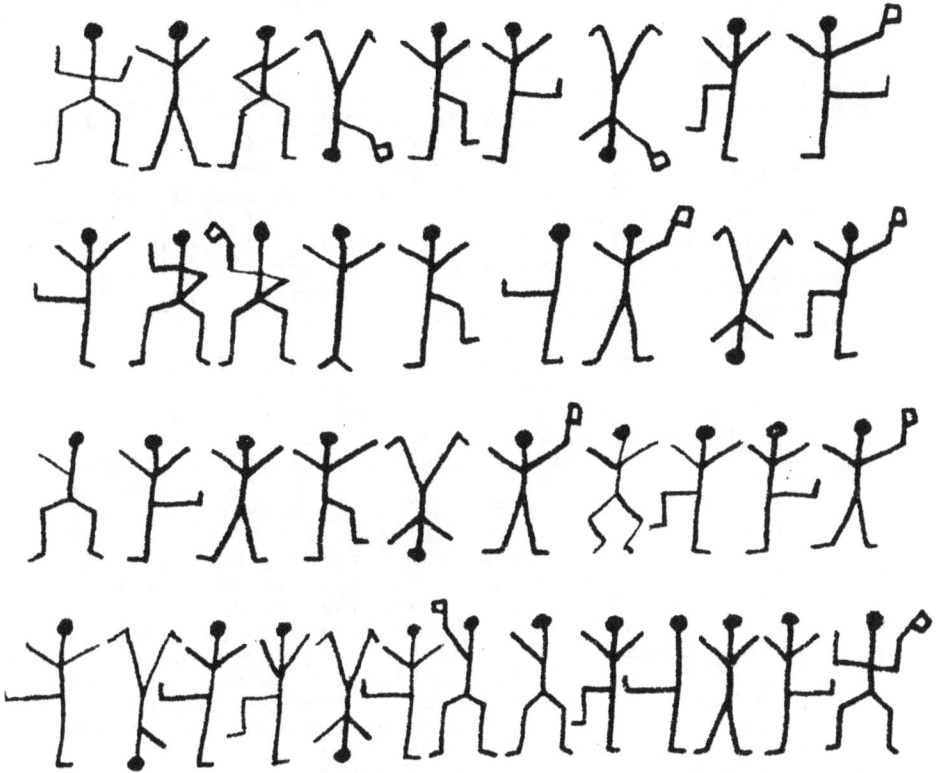

Volume 1   Number 4
July 1977

THE MYSTERY FANCIER

Volume 1 Number 4
July 1977

TABLE OF CONTENTS

Subscription rates: $7.50 per year (6 issues) US; $9.00 overseas; single issue price $1.50.

The MYSTERY FANcier is edited and published by Guy M. Town-
send, 1256 Pidgeon Perch Lane, Memphis, TN 38116 USA.
Deadline for September issue: 1 August 1977.

MYSTERIOUSLY SPEAKING . . .

To state the obvious, *TMF* has changed its format. The day after I took the last issue to the post office I received a phone call from one of the employees of that mysterious organization, who informed me that the magazine did not qualify for book rate, but that the post office would be happy to handle the magazine at third class rate; all I had to do was pay an extra 25¢ per copy. I said thanks anyway and went down and picked them all up. I had mailed the three previous issues at a different post office without difficulty, so I drove immediately from one post office to the other and re-mailed the magazines, this time without a hitch. But the incident set me to thinking. I knew from conversations with other amateur publishers that the post office was somewhat fickle on the subject, but not having had any problems before I had not thought much about it. Now, however, it was forcibly brought home to me that the post office was a potential source of inconvenience and expense to me, and I bit my nails for a while considering the problem. To cut a long story short, I finally came up with the present format, which enables me to print sixty pages on fifteen sheets which, together with the single sheet of cover stock, comes to just under three ounces and can be mailed first class domestically for 35¢. (Given the outrageous cost of air mail overseas, I will continue to try to sneak copies to overseas subscribers at book rate; air mailing this issue to England, for example, would cost $1.02.) This is more than it cost to mail the old format book rate, but I save money on paper and ink. The fixed costs are about the same. The earlier issues were for the most part typed directly on to stencils at a cost of about 30¢ each. In producing this issue, however, I typed the copy onto regular paper, had the copy photo reduced at a cost of 30¢ per double page, and then made electro-stencils of the reduced copy at about 50¢ per double page. Changing to this format has enabled me to reduce the production cost per issue slightly, even with the increased cost of mailing the issues out first class.

The new format is not without its shortcomings, however, the most obvious one being that it is harder to read. I experimented with varying degrees of reduction before settling on this one. The pages of this issue have the same number of lines as the earlier issues, though I had to reduce the number of characters per line by about 20% in order to squeeze two pages onto a single sheet. The size of the characters is comparable to those of *Baker Street Miscellanea*, for those of you who subscribe to that worthy publication. Despite this, *BSM* is easier to read than *TMF*, because it is offset printed while this is mimeographed.

So there you are. I hope that you will agree that the pluses of the change offset the minuses. On the minus side we have a slight reduction in words per page (and, potentially, per issue as well, since the maximum page count is still sixty) and somewhat fuzzier copy. On the plus side we have faster and more secure delivery via first class mail (which will give you more time to respond to an issue before the next deadline), a smaller, more convenient size (you can

open it flat or stick it in your pocket or purse, which you
could not do with the larger issues), and an editor who is
no longer being persecuted by the post office. And there is
another plus. In the past some of you have complained about
the absence of ads in *TMF*. I have not run them because it
was my understanding that the inclusion of ads would render
TMF ineligible for fourth class postage rates. That objection no longer applies, so henceforth ads will be accepted
for *TMF* at the following rates: full page (6" wide x 9½"
long *maximum* dimensions) $5.00; half page (6 x 4½) $3.00;
quarter page (6 x 2) $2.00; shorter ads, up to six lines (6
x 1) $1.00. All ads should be camera ready, except for the
small $1.00 ads, which I will retype. These prices are
based on what it will cost to add another sheet to the issue
once the sixty page (fifteen sheet) maximum has been reached.
Extra postage alone will amount to about $15.00 at current
subscription levels, so I don't think these prices are out
of line. If *TMF* consistently has more than four pages of
ads it will be possible to lower the price for multi-page
ads (probably to $2.50 for second and each additional page).

I continue to hope for an increase in contributions to
TMF. Even the letters section of this issue is embarrassing-
ly short, and I'm running out of rabbits to pull out of my
hat. What I would do without the faithful few who contribute to virtually every issue I do not even like to contem-
plate.

Mailing #16 of DAPA-EM arrived today, and on the cover
is the "Official Secret Decoder" for the Dancing Men code.
I add this note to tell you all that I worked out the mess-
age on the cover of *TMF* 1:4 more than a week ago. Not that
it really matters, but I thought my cover was kind of cute
and I didn't want you to think I had cribbed the idea from
Art Scott.

(Continued from page 60) *Don Markstein pointed out, when
that segment of the Saga first appeared in DAPA-EM, that
chitterlings is pronounced "chitlins", which, as I remarked
to him, "rather effectively takes the wind out of my sails.
In my defense I can only lamely point out that a purist like
Wolfe whould stick with first spellings (if we can hold
Wolfe responsible for Stout's [Archie's] spelling) and that,
however it is pronounced, 'pig chitlins' is still redundant."
Finally, I have no objection whatever to southern accents
per se (I speak with one myself); it is the deliberate,
"honey-chile" distortions to which I object. Southerners
speak with an accent; they don't (except in a very few, very
isolated areas) speak a separate dialect.]*

THE MYSTERIES OF THE PSEUDONYMOUS PROFESSORS
By Joseph Barbato

Few things seem to win an academic the disapproval of colleagues as quickly as the writing of popular fiction. Small wonder, then, that many academics write thrillers, mysteries, and other fiction under pseudonyms, thereby enjoying both professorial dignity and, sometimes, commercial literary success.

"Trevanian," for instance, continues to teach at a university in the Southwest while writing such best-selling novels as *The Eiger Sanction* and *The Main.*

Others, including Erich Segal (who wrote *Love Story* while on the faculty of Yale), have put their own names on popular novels. Some have soon found themselves unemployed.

Attitudes vary, of course, from campus to campus; but an untenured faculty member is still wise to consider the anonymity of a pseudonym. The case is well put in Hubert Monteilhet's recent novel, *Murder at the Frankfurt Book Fair.* The protagonist, a Sorbonne professor who writes thrillers under a pseudonym, says:

"Notorious homosexuality would probably get me promoted. But scribbling thrillers doesn't impress anyone; it's not authentic enough, not sufficiently committed. . . . If by any misfortune I was ever found out, my colleagues would make fun of me."

For all that, academics continue to write popular fiction, including such mystery novels as *The Question of Max* and *Promised Land.* Why do they do it? Robin Winks, professor of history at Yale and a reviewer of mysteries for *The New Republic,* thinks long, cold winters on New England campuses may have something to do with it.

"In any event, most mysteries by academics are not very good," says Mr. Winks. "They're often filled with boring talk that's unrealistic even to academic readers."

A mystery addict since the age of 10, Mr. Winks adds that many historians both relax and work by reading detective fiction. "The thought processes of a detective and a historian are similar. Besides, mystery fiction romanticizes the historian's kind of activity."

Of course, whatever their reasons, academics have long been known to keep mysteries on their night tables. But *writing* them? Mr. Winks agrees that many professors are working in the genre, and notes that several of his colleagues at Yale write for the mystery magazines--under pseudonyms.

"There's definitely the notion that you should use a pseudonym," he says.

Unfortunately, even a pen name can have its perils, as "Amanda Cross" learned in 1964 when her first mystery, *In the Last Analysis,* was nominated for an award for the best first mystery by the Mystery Writers of America. "I was terrified that I would win," says the author. As it turned out, Harry Kemelman took the prize with his first novel, *Friday the Rabbi Slept Late*, and the identity of "Amanda Cross" remained a secret.

Her real name is Carolyn Heilbrun, and she is a professor of English at Columbia University. In 1964, though, she was new to Columbia's faculty and concerned that publication of a mystery novel would adversely affect a forthcoming decision on her tenure.

In the years since, she has produced several other mysteries--*The James Joyce Murder*, *Poetic Justice*, *The Theban Mysteries*, and her new one, *The Question of Max*.

Even today Ms. Heilbrun is reluctant to discuss her work as a mystery writer. A quiet, scholarly person, she is clearly more comfortable as the author of *Toward a Recognition of Androgyny*, as the editor of *Lady Ottline's Album*, and as president of the Virginia Woolf Society. She is on leave from Columbia this year with a Rockefeller Foundation humanities fellowship.

Ms. Heilbrun nonetheless takes her mystery writing quite seriously. In a recent issue of *The American Scholar*, she wrote, "Detective fiction is written and read by so intelligent and accomplished a group of people precisely because the detective's work is, above all, that of an imaginative artist."

As a reader, her own favorite mystery writers include P. D. James, Ngaio Marsh, Rex Stout, and Dorothy Sayers. "I started writing mysteries because I missed the books of Dorothy Sayers and decided to write my own," she says.

Ms. Heilbrun believes that the Sayers books are "superbly constructed detective plots, played out in witty comedies of manners"; and, indeed, much the same might be said of her own series of novels about Kate Fansler, a professor of English and amateur sleuth. Ms. Heilbrun has become a master of what the mystery critic Anthony Boucher called "the leisurely and witty academic mystery novel."

As their titles indicate, Ms. Heilbrun's books have a decidedly "literary" cast: James Joyce's work was central to *The James Joyce Murder*, and the poetry of W. H. Auden served to inspire *Poetic Justice*. In *The Question of Max* there has been a murder involving the estate of a famous English novelist, and Kate Fansler becomes embroiled in an adventure that takes her from Maine to Oxford, England. A university colleague, Max Reston, is very much involved in it all.

A suspenseful and entertaining tale, *Max* is marred by much dialogue that is too "academic" for its own good (*e.g.*, "Solitude is comprehensible, though it has devastating effects upon one's conversation: have you ever noticed that the solitary, when they do see you, positively bubble over with talk, the pressure, no doubt, of all the ideas which have for so long gone unuttered?"). Fans of Dorothy Sayers, for whom erudition and intellectuality are the overriding considerations, will most certainly find the book to their liking.

At the opposite end of the mystery genre, there is the hard-boiled detective fiction of Robert B. Parker, associate professor of English at Northeastern University. The author of two textbooks and a member of the editorial board of

Studies in American Fiction, he is better known to mystery readers for his books *The Godwulf Manuscript, God Save the Child, Mortal Stakes,* and, most recently, *Promised Land.*

Mr. Parker, who held a variety of writing and teaching jobs before joining Northeastern in 1968, has based his series on a character called Spenser, a Boston private eye reminiscent of Raymond Chandler's Philip Marlowe. His reason for taking up mystery writing is remarkably similar to Ms. Heilbrun's.

"I missed Philip Marlowe so much that I thought I'd invent my own," says Mr. Parker, whose doctoral dissertation concerned the novels of Dashiell Hammett, Raymond Chandler, and Ross Macdonald. "I was raised on the stuff. Marlowe gave me my idea of what manhood was."

Mr. Parker teaches creative writing and a course on "The Novel of Violence" at Northeastern. Like his fictional detective, he is a weight-lifter and a gourmet cook.

Of the mystery novel, Mr. Parker says: "It's a form as rigid as the sonnet. I like that. It allows me to do and say things that other forms don't allow."

Mindful that much of American fiction has been about men without women, Mr. Parker in each of his books involved his tough-guy hero in a deepening relationship with a young woman named Susan Silverman.

"I'm trying to work out some fictional patterns that one rarely finds in American fiction," the author explains. "I want to write about love. I want to see if the American hero can be complete. If he can be a whole man without losing the values of childhood. If he can move into an adulthood that includes the power to love as well as the power to kill."

So, much to the consternation of his publisher and some writer-friends, Mr. Parker's *Promised Land* offers not only a tale about murder, extortion, bank robbery, and the search for a runaway wife, but also the prospect that Spenser, the gutsy, beer-drinking hero, may soon get married.

In a scene near the end of the novel, Spencer says, "I don't belong out there, Suze," referring to the town where Susan Silverman lives.

"Of course you don't," she replies. "Look at you. You are the ultimate man, the ultimate adult in some ways, the great powerful protecting father. And yet you are the biggest goddamned kid I ever saw. You would have no business in the suburbs, in a Cape Cod house, cutting the lawn, having a swim at the club. I mean you once strangled a man to death, did you not?"

"Yeah, name was Phil. Never knew his other name, just Phil. I didn't like it."

Unaware of Parker's experiment, most readers undoubtedly approach his books as conventional detective fare. On that basis, the novels certainly offer far better writing and characterizations than most private-eye mysteries.

But surely his associates at Northeastern appreciate what Mr. Parker is up to? "I don't think many of them read my books," he says. In fact, he adds, many of his fellow teachers are either amused or suspicious about his celebrity as a mystery writer.

Mr. Parker has never made secret his authorship of the

Spenser series. The books have appeared under his real name
since the first one came out in 1974.
    Earlier that year, he had been granted tenure.

THE WIT AND WISDOM OF THE MYSTERY STORY:

QUOTATIONS FROM THE MYSTERIES--PART IV

BY MARVIN LACHMAN

Allingham, Margery

Flowers for the Judge (1936) "Even his car is denied him: the fog is too thick. So he walks. He takes refuge in the time-honored escape which men of every age and every generation have used to soothe their troubled spirits."

The Fashion in Shrouds (1938) "That is the difference between the world of my youth and the world of today. then I was bored because nothing could happen; now I am apprehensive because nothing couldn't."

Tether's End (1958) Inspector Luke re Parliament eliminating the death penalty: "I neither like it nor dis-like it. Once I've delivered the man to the court, I reckon my busi-ness is done. I'm the dog. I bring in the bird. I don't expect to have to cook him."

Cargo of Eagles (1968) Re Inspector Oates who "had risen from the ranks and never suffered from a fear of heights."

NOTE: Re the reading of mysteries, Margery Allingham once said: "If you have an intelligent mind and you like to read, and you need to escape, then you require an intelligent lit-erature of escape."

Ames, Delano

She Shall Have Murder (1949) "The trouble in this case is that people sometimes tell the truth, and that confuses us."

Ballinger, Bill

Portrait in Smoke (1950) "The walls to all the rooms were so thin that the only privacy you had was sitting around with your own thoughts."

Bennett, Margot

The Man Who Didn't Fly (1955) 1. "Morgan's got so much anxiety in his heart he walks with a list to the left side."
2. "You come here . . . to see how the rich live. You are a welfare worker in reverse."
3. "Desperate fancies and premoni-tions bred in her mind like bacteria

8

in an open wound. She lay in agony, trying somehow to find the strength to control her own thoughts."

Beste, R. Vernon   *The Moonbeams* (1961) "He did not mind the winter. It was autumn which always depressed him deeply. For him, the prospect of death was harder to bear than death itself."

Blochman, Lawrence G.   "Dr. Coffee and the Pardell Case" (*EQMM* 6/72) "He was more of a sadist than the Marquis himself."

Boucher, Anthony   *The Case of the Solid Key* (1941) "Who was it said it's easy to believe the impossible but never the implausible?"

Buchan, John   *The Power House* (1913) "You think a wall as solid as the earth separates civilization from barbarism. I tell you the division is a thread, a sheet of glass. A touch here, a push there, and you bring back the reign of Satan."

Canning, Victor   *The House of the Seven Flies* (1952) "What a life it must be if you spent half your time refereeing a fight between your desires and your conscience."

Chesterton, G. K.   (Sources unknown) 1. "If a thing is worth doing, it is worth doing badly." 2. "An adventure is only an inconvenience rightly considered."

Gault, William Campbell   *The Canvas Coffin* (1953) "The wrong people have all the money because the right people have the wrong appetites."
Sweet Wild Wench (1959) Private Eye Joe Puma: "I have to work with thieves and fools and politicians and pimps and religious fanatics. I have to work with people and that takes a strong stomach."

Gilbert, Michael   *Overdrive* (1967) " . . . a thin, sad Cockney with a face like a long list of home-and-away defeats."

Gottlieb, Kathryn   "The Gun" (*EQMM* 1/71) "Elsinore is the kind of town where if you want to stay over-night, you have to buy a house."

Hillerman, Tony   *The Fly on the Wall* (1971) "Some famous writer once said when asked if he had any advice for the aspiring writer: 'Always remember the shiny side of the carbon paper has to face away from you.'"

Lyons, Arthur   *All God's Children* (1975) Re an expensive restaurant: "The check was more sobering than the coffee."

McCloy, Helen   *Unfinished Crime* (1954) Heroine when asked whether she is tough-minded or tender-minded replies: "I hope William James would class me with the tough-minded, though I'm sure Mickey Spillane would not."

Macdonald, Ross   *The Underground Man* (1971) A grown-up says, "We're losing a whole generation. They're punishing us for bringing them into the world."

McGivern, William P.   *Very Cold for May* (1950) A character who is noted for keeping his sex drive in check says, "I'm not called the North American continent for nothing."

MacInnes, Helen   *While Still We Live* (1944) "What was the process of becoming old but a choosing of the essential things, a discarding of too many impulses, a forgetting of too many dreams?"

Millar, Margaret   *Ask for Me Tomorrow* (1976) A fat police detective says, "I dislike all forms of exercise except that of the imagination. From the neck up I am very athletic."

Queen, Ellery   *A Fine and Private Place* (1971) "Nobody in the publishing profession pays any attention whatever to a mystery writer except when banking the profits from his mean endeavors. We're the ditch diggers of literature."

Reilly, Helen   *Follow Me* (1962) "The city wore an air of mourning after the holidays. It was a disgruntled and disillusioned giant that slept after the turn of the year, with nothing immediately ahead but bad weather and income taxes."

Sayers, Dorothy L.   *Clouds of Witness* (1926) "Facts are

10

like cows. If you look them in the
face hard enough they generally run
away."
Busman's Honeymoon (1937) Re attor-
neys: "They also serve who only serve
writs."

Watson, Colin

Snobbery With Violence (1971, non-
fiction) 1. Re mysteries as two-
dimensional fiction: "It could not
have offered what it did--relaxation,
diversion, reassurance--if it had
possessed that third dimension which
gives a story power to affect the
reader in much the same way as actual experience."
2. Definition of a permissive society: " . . . a society less convinced
than formerly that morals, like
drains, were matters for public ad-
ministration. . . . "

Stout, Rex

Too Many Detectives (1960) Nero
Wolfe: "Like doctors, lawyers,
plumbers, and many others, I get my
income from the necessities, the
tribulations, and the misfortunes of
my fellow beings."

Tey, Josephine

Miss Pym Disposes (1946) ". . . producing another of her unhelpful of-
ferings. She's like someone running
round with black-currant lozenges to
the victims of an earthquake."

Williams, Charles

Girl Out Back (1958) Regarding an
insistent questioner: "Torquemada
lost a good man when Otis blundered
into the wrong century."

THE PROGRAMMED WRITING OF DEAN R. KOONTZ

BY GEORGE KELLEY

I've followed Dean R. Koontz's writing career since the late 1960's when he was turning out tons of science fiction. He diversified, writing caper novels under the name of Brian Coffey, and suspense novels under the K. R. Dwyer pseudonym.

But the key to Koontz's writing is his guide to beginning authors: *Writing Genre Fiction* (Writer's Digest, 1972). In this enormously fascinating text, Koontz shares the secret that made him a successful writer. Essentially, there are key conventions to every genre; by mastering the formulae, a diligent writer can produce a salable manuscript.

Koontz produced the best writer's handbook I'd ever read. But something bothered me about the book. Only when I read *Night Chills* and *Dragonfly* (as by K. R. Dwyer) did that nagging point produce so much irritation that I could seize it and study it.

Koontz's situation is similar to that when a favorite writer runs out of steam and begins to write the same book over and over again: the situation Ross Macdonald finds himself in. Koontz's situation is a little different; each book seems to be too formulated, too mechanical. The result, in each case, is staleness.

Dragonfly (Random, 1975; Ballantine, 1976) is a mixture of a "doomsday" book and a "conspiracy" novel. Within the CIA is a supersecret group that plans to take over the country. They plan a diversion by setting off an artificially produced plague to kill the political and social elite in Peking, allowing for the Nationalists on Formosa to retake the mainland in the confusion. The second part of the plan is the assassination of the President and top political leaders until a politician controlled by The Committee can take over the top spot.

The book has two subplots: the search for the young Chinese who unknowingly carries the surgically implanted capsule of the deadly plague and the search for those top officials who are secretly involved in The Committee's conspiracy.

There's lots of action and suspense, but somehow the effect is lessened because we've read it all before, somewhere. The ending is unsatisfactory because Koontz has The Good Guys quietly assassinating The Bad Guys. I'll come back to the unsatisfactory ending later in this review.

Night Chills (Atheneum, 1976; Fawcett, 1977) features a mad scientist who discovers techniques of subliminal perception that allow him to completely control most people. He takes his idea to a millionaire who's a religious fanatic, the millionaire sees the mind control techniques as a way to stamp out evil in the world and to make himself a sort of High Priest of the World. The millionaire draws in a corrupt General who's the security chief for the Northeast to complete the partnership. So we have the archtypes: mad scientist, power-hungry millionaire, and corrupt General. Sound familiar?

The mind control techniques need to be field tested

before the three can use it to take over a Middle East country as their first step to taking over the world. Sound familiar?

They pick a small logging town in Maine, Black River, because of its isolation. They have the mind control drug dumped into the reservoir, the population programmed with subliminals hidden in TV programs. Then the mad scientist comes to town to study the effect.

The mad scientist is also very kinky sexually. During one of the more graphic scenes in the book, a young boy who is unaffected by the mind control drugs, breaks into the session and has to be killed. His father, sister, father's lover and her father, also unaffected by the drugs, discover the body and the plot. We then have a series of scenes reminiscent of the terrifying movie (and book by Jack Finny) *Invasion of the Body Snatchers*.

But we get another unsatisfying ending with The Good Guys killing The Bad Guys and then destroying all information on the mind control technique (the world isn't ready for it). Sound Familiar?

That gets us back to the question of endings in *Night Chills* and *Dragonfly*. In each book we have an unsatisfactory ending: in *Dragonfly* the Good Guys adopt the amoral assassination tactics of the Bad Guys in order to wipe out the Bad Guys. But doesn't that make them Bad Guys? And the solution doesn't involve solving the problem, but destroying the problem.

It's the same in *Night Chills*: the Bad Guys get wiped out by the Good Guys, and the Good Guys handle the problem of the existence of mind control techniques by destroying the information. Again, not solving the problem, but destroying the problem. The resorting to extra-legal solutions, while neat, lets the reader down and produces a phony sensation, a hollow feeling at the conclusion of the book.

Don't get me wrong, these books are good entertainment. But the motive behind writing this review is to come to grips with the irritation programmed writing produces. Koontz follows his cookbook formula faithfully. That's what bothers me. Koontz is a better writer than that. His *Surrounded* (written under the Brian Coffey pseudonym, Bobbs-Merrill, 1974) is a brilliant caper novel. Koontz was able to transcend the conventions in that book.

Unfortunately, Koontz seems trapped by his conventions, his formulae, in *Night Chills* and *Dragonfly*. That's the irritation that nagged me while I was reading these books: I kept saying, "Dean, you can do better, much better, than this."

FURTHER EXCURSIONS INTO THE WACKY WORLD OF
HARRY STEPHEN KEELER
By Art Scott

(Reprinted, with permission,
from *Shot Scott's Rap Sheet* #5)

For this installment of "Dumbfounded in Keelerland" I
sent out copies of assorted Keeler titles for review to several friends who expressed an interest in experiencing Keeler firsthand. Most "virgins" where HSK is concerned, I
think you'll find their reviews most entertaining. I've provided some commentary and a couple of reviews of my own.
Shall we proceed?

GETTING AWAY WITH LITERARY MURDER: An Awestruck Dwight Decker Reviews *The Face of the Man from Saturn*.
    If a high school-aged science-fiction fan with social-
ist leanings and a lot of time on his hands were to try his
hand at writing a mystery novel, *The Face of the Man from
Saturn* is what he might come up with. People that don't
quite act like people, dialogue that somehow doesn't ring
true, plot developments like bunnies out of a hat, a longish
essay on economics plopped right in the middle from out of
nowhere, and some of the clumsiest writing ever published
outside of the vanity press--that's this book, all right.
    Yet, as mysteries go, it seems to be pretty straight-
forward, at least compared to some of the other volumes in
the HSK collection. There are no mathematical geniuses
named Quiribus, no strange circuses holed up in even stranger towns, no Supercopters--just a reporter named Jimmy Kentland working for a Socialist newspaper in Chicago, the *Sun*.
    And it starts out normally enough. Kentland has been
working for the *Sun* for a week, and a combination of bad
luck and circumstance has contributed to his loss of a couple of scoops for the paper, which sits none too well with
his editor. That worthy, about to embark on a sudden trip
to Cincinatti to buy another newspaper, tells Kentland he
has a week to come up with a hot scoop. To top that off,
because the night editor is home with gastric cramps and his
normal substitute is on vacation, Kentland has to man the
city desk until 3:00 AM. There's also the matter of a
slightly peculiar free-lance military affairs writer due to
drop his column off at 9:00 PM, but that's easily handled.
Then, at a little after two in the morning, a messenger boy
delivers an illiterate note which claims that at 1710 Crilly
Court exists "something strange and startling wat no other
paper has got. This is bony fidy." Kentland is off and running, and so is *The Face of the Man from Saturn*.
    And that's when things start to become darned peculiar.
As a policeman says a little later, "There's scrooey work
here to-night. . . ." A girl is run down by Kentland's cab
on the way to Crilly Court--rather coincidentally, too,
since her role in the plot is considerable and her enforced
period of silence during her stay in the hospital keeps the

book from ending 200 pages early. 1710 Crilly Court turns
out to be a curiosity shop run by an eccentric Persian named
Abdul Mazurka who may be involved in drug traffic. Or rather, the late eccentric Persian named Abdul Mazurka. Kentland arrives to find him dead, apparently murdered by a
spear appropriated from a suit of medieval armor in the shop.
Strangest of all is a painting in the shop:

> Kentland's eye came to rest on a peculiar thing.
> Held in a massive gilt frame was an oil painting
> that measured, perhaps, two feet by a foot and a
> half. A signature in bright red, in the lower
> right hand corner read, simply: "Durri," and the
> words neatly painted in black on the lower left
> hand corner, proclaimed the title: "Man from
> Saturn." That it was one of those bizarre
> paintings to be found here and there in every
> collection and in every art studio was evident.
> The green-taloned hand with seven fingers that
> seemed to be reaching up to clutch the frame was
> never hand of man or beast on earth. That the
> painting was that of the face--the supposed face--
> of an extremely fantastic being was also patent,
> for the tips of the two speckled brown horns
> stretched almost to the top of the frame. But
> the surprising thing--indeed the startling
> thing--about it was that the painting had been
> mutilated by a sharp roundabout cut, and all
> that now remained was a wide fringe of canvas
> and a black, gaping hole which must at one time
> have presented the face of the "Man from Saturn."

Monstrous as that painting may sound, it later develops that
there are *two* of the things . . . .

It all makes perfect sense by the end of the book--per-
fectly screwy sense--after a couple hundred pages of rushing
around, leads, hints, phoned-in tips, and third order ratio-
cination. The plot is an incredible web of characters and
events, ranging from an old, half-forgotten treason case in
France to a recent but aborted conspiracy of Anarcho-Commun-
ists to blow up the offices of the *Times-Star*, a conserva-
tive Chicago paper. Abdul Mazurka is just the tip of the
iceberg.

But by far one of the most bizarre elements of *The Face
of the Man from Saturn* is chapter XII, "The Strange Story of
John Jones' Dollar," a political-economic satire set in the
year 3235. Its only real relevance to the plot is the fact
that the same typewriter used to write it was used to write
something else--but there it is, a twenty-odd paged lump of
hilarious irrelevancy gratuitously dropped amid a mystery
novel. I wouldn't be surprised if it were written separate-
ly and for other purposes, and written into *The Face of the
Man from Saturn* as an afterthought. Readers of science-fiction will find Harry Stephen Keeler's version of the 33rd
century astonishing, to say the least.

All ends happily. Besides a new and better job, Jimmy
Kentland also gets a wife out of the merrie doings once the
dust has settled. The courtship is short and preposterous
in the madcap HSK fashion. Kentland falls in love with the
girl because of her "appealing brown eyes," and tells her:

"I've actually met the counterpart of the dream-girl that
has been in my mind for years." The book concludes with
these tender lines:

"The parlour of an undertaking establishment,"
he said, gravely, "is a queer place to begin romance in, but--"

He drew her to him and kissed her on her warm,
red lips.

Surely there is something that must be said about a
writer who can compose a line like "'The parlour of an undertaking establishment,' he said gravely . . ." and not real-
ize how weirdly absurd it is, but I'm not sure what!

Harry Stephen Keeler . . . one of a kind.

[*The Face of the Man from Saturn*: Dutton, 1933. British
title: *The Crilly Court Mystery*: Ward, Lock, 1933.

Dwight Decker is a polyglot multitalent, whose witty
and thoughtful commentaries have brightened comics and
science-fiction fandom for some years now. Dwight has written Bugs Bunny stories, translated Perry Rhodan novels, con-
sorted with political odd ducks--working at sf freelancing
when he has a spare moment. He's currently living in Keeler's beloved London of the West, doing his bit for Socialism
by working for the U.S. Government (sorry, Doc, I couldn't
resist). On a recent visit to an old Chicago bookseller,
he reports: "This guy *knew* Keeler--he patronized his shop on
occasion. 'Bit of an odd duck . . . bought the strangest
books,' he mused." I'll just bet he did! A.S.]

Dale Nelson recounts his encounter with *The Five Silver
Buddhas*.

I didn't finish Harry Keeler's *The Five Silver Buddhas*.
Two-thirds or so of the way through, I decided not to go on.

The problem is that I simply don't have a taste for
"whodunits," which is what this is, as opposed to *some* interest in "detective stories," which are stories about detectives, like Peter Wimsey or Sherlock Holmes. Keeler's story,
as far as I got, was almost all puzzle. His characterizations are cardboard, with hardly any relation to reality.
Keeler's characters are like the people in old crime comics--
which no doubt accounts for part of Art's enjoyment.

Now this matter of characterization (and setting)
shouldn't be considered a defect. Those of us who are more
interested in that sort of thing are simply in the wrong
place. You don't go to Taco Bell for chop suey. Keeler was
writing a story with an (apparently) very convoluted pattern:
the repeated references to webs reflect this. The game, of
course, is to grasp the pattern before the author reveals it
to you. But this is a game I lack the patience, or aptitude,
to play.

I ought to make clear that it's not as though Keeler
wrote a story without any life, just an intellectual puzzle.
He gets across a rather distinct *texture* through his nerve
in presenting some ludicrous dialog and coincidences. Let
me give you an example of a Keeler character's speech:

(The dialect of Tano, a Japanese butler)
It ees, Mestair Harding, a rep'sentation of Buddha ·
--and ees a Chinese piece. . . . I do not myself

ridd Chinese--so I cannot tell you whether the
character [on the Buddha's stomach] means--kosher?
--The eegn'rant Chinese to soch a fine race like
we Japs--for we consider the Chinese mongrel dogs,
fit to do but as you say your friend do--iron
shirts--yes they believe impleecitly that images
of Buddha breeng luck. Now me, I am American-
born [!!!] Japan' am myself beyon' soch supersti-
tious state. As are my own people back in Nippon.

Or consider this eye-opening discourse by the hero's girl-
friend:

For it has been evident for several weeks, you
see, Penn, that all the necessary trials, checking
and tests would be over by this date. And Cron,
according to his contract, has drawn up a complete,
detailed outline of the whole method, with all its
mathematical equations, its theories about the
atomic changes in the red hot steel when subjected
to vibration, the reorganization of the atoms when
these high-penetrating rays pass between their in-
terstices, as well as all the practical sketches of
the curves used on the cams that are on the vibrating mechanisms, to the very type of gas and elec-
trodes in the ray-producing tube. The full method,
in fact, of applying all this to hot steel, including the combinations for the proper fusing of the
actions of the vibrating cams--in case, Penn, you
know what a cam is--for I'm afraid I don't. [!!!!!!]
Whew!

Whomever you have been reading, I can nearly guarantee
that Harry Stephen Keeler will be a change of pace.

[*The Five Silver Buddhas*: Dutton, 1935.

Well, you can't please everyone. Dale Nelson, you may
remember, is the perpetrator of the "Shylock Hames" parodies
which appeared in these pages in issues past. He hails from
Oregon, where his reading tastes run more to the likes of
Tolkien, Chesterton, and Rider Haggard.

I might add a bit more information as to what *Five Silver Buddhas* is all about. . . . Like *Sing Sing Nights*, to
be discussed later on, it is in part made up of Keeler's magazine stories (including his first published tale, "Victim
No. 5," about a strangler who gets his just desserts). The
stories are worked into the framework of the novel by inter-
cessions of the Buddhas, which, as we learn eventually, are
very much *mo-sei-gei*, i.e., bad luck charms. Four of the
people who obtain them at an auction--like the strangler,
one Ivan Kossakoff--come to unhappy ends. The typical Keelerian hero, Penn Harding, has a buddha as well, and the *mo-
sei-gei* indeed seems to be working overtime, as Penn is accused of stealing the astounding steelmaking formula described above from the safe of his betrothed's father.

In the end, however, it all works out for the best,
thanks to the law of *"Tzei gwon kei cheng."* Keeler's talent
for cannibalizing his old stories and levering them into a
new web is very much in evidence in this book, as is his
fascination for things exotic and Oriental.

I should say here that Dale's supposition that the mystery is solvable in the usual way of "fair-play" mysteries is incorrect, despite Dutton's insistence on making a "challenge to the reader" in the middle of the book. Keeler did not construct his plots in that fashion, as will I think be made clear in the next review. A.S.]

SKULL DAZE: Ron Harris examines *The Riddle of the Travelling Skull* and *The Skull of the Waltzing Clown*.

In *The Mystery Writer's Handbook*, Harry Stephen Keeler described his favorite "trick of the mystery trade": "Have a character serve as red herring for the real red herring in the story!" That Keeler practiced what he preached is amply illustrated in *The Riddle of the Traveling Skull* and *The Skull of the Waltzing Clown*, two dandy volumes from the Harry Stephen Keeler library of zaniness.

Though I'm reviewing the two novels together, the books are unrelated in content. They are not, like some other Keelers, segments of a multivolume "meganovel." But they share much more than just a skull in the title. Both are prime examples of the outrageously complicated plotting and batty characters which make Keeler a delight to read.

Keeler called his peculiar form of the novel a "webwork novel." However, his books resemble spiderwebs less than they do a cable which has been twisted backward and partly unravelled. On one side of the twist the cable is a solid mass, but this branches out into a number of component strands, each of which divides further into several more. Then, this maze of individual threads reforms cluster by cluster into a single piece. Similarly, the central thread of a Keeler novel blossoms forth into a bewildering array of intersecting plots, characters and coincidence. Then, slowly, inexorably, every string is twined into an ingenious resolution which accounts for every last piece.

The Riddle of the Travelling Skull, written in 1934, concerns the first-person adventures of one Clay Calthorpe. Calthorpe is the typical Keeler hero: a breezy, slang-talking young Chicagoan who in movies might have been played by Lee Tracy. Calthorpe is returning from an overseas business trip to resume his duties with the Pelton Confectionary Company, makers of "the most marvelously hued purple jelly beans ever munched by a king." Clay is anticipating a nice raise and a pending marriage to the boss's daughter. Instead, the chance acquisition of a singular human skull throws him into the middle of a twenty-year-old mystery of murder and blackmail involving--among others!--such diverse elements as Milo Payne, the mysterious Cockney with the Sherlockholmesian cap; the Great Simon and his 2163 pearl buttons; Abigail Sprigge, the elusive poetess who may or may not be O. M. Lee; John Barr and his Barr Bag, with the exclusive Billy Bulger Bulge; Ichabod Chang, the scripture-quoting Chinese killer; missionary Sophie Kratzenschneiderwümpel, a.k.a. "Suing Sophie"; Philodexter Maxillus, the man destined to publish the country's first commercially-successful poetry magazine . . . but that's only the beginning. Every seeming irrelevance is tied into a neat package which leaves the reader's own skull spinning.

The Skull of the Waltzing Clown, written the next year, consists largely of a conversation between shirt-salesman

George Stannard and his Uncle Simon, a wealthy power broker
who owns *7-Tales Magazine* and collects antique safes. George
is offered an opportunity to repay an old debt by engaging
in a bit of shady business for Uncle Simon. Before the matter is resolved, he has felt the influences of Van Hymes
Severingham Cushing-Barkley, the eccentric *7-Tales* editor;
Titus G. Fenwick, the Canadian card shark; Pau-Ho, an Oriental drug which gives its victim 20 days' sleep followed by 37
days' amnesia; Lucifer Zull, shady villain from the past;
"The Rebel," a nameless girl with a hatred of all Babbitts
and shirt salesmen; O Lilly Sing Lee, an Oklahoma author
with a name the origin of which makes for the most preposterous and fascinating tales of all time; and of course
Clowno, the Waltzing Fool, whose topmost member is destined
for a strange fate. By the time the reader reaches the final surprise--located, naturally, on the last page--the entire fabric of space and time has been ripped up and resewn
a dozen times.

I've used the word "coincidence" several times in de-
scribing Keeler's books, but "coincidence" is a bad choice
of nouns. In fact, nothing in an HSK book happens by chance.
The Keeler universe is governed by the workings of an omni-
potent and very particular Fate which manifests itself in
the Law of Karma, or the Lawa of Cross and Re-Cross. In
this world scheme, every wrong is somehow redressed in an
appropriate manner, no matter how long it takes; and every
good is rewarded as is fitting. In short, all those whose
paths cross must eventually cross again! This underlying
Truth motivates every Keeler book (and is occasionally spelt
out, as it is in *Waltzing Clown*). What seems at first to be
a string of outlandish coincidences is really an inevitable
progression of planned circumstances guaranteeing the cause
of cosmic justice.

Consequently it's impossible to relate the plote of a
Keeler mystery without giving away the ending. Plot and
ending are so interdependent that the two cannot exist sep-
arately. Furthermore, Keeler mysteries aren't really mysteries in the traditional sense. Here is no sporting collection of facts and clues allowing the more clever reader
to solve the mystery himself.

This fact obviously bewildered the editor of the "Dutton Clue Mysteries," publisher of these two volumes. Series
format demanded a standard page to be inserted at a key
point in the story, admonishing the reader to stop and review the facts, then to decide on a solution before reading
the remainder of the book. But *nobody* could come close to
solving a Keeler mystery, even after "all the characters and
clues have been presented." The editor made a game try in
Waltzing Clown, asking for a decision on page 107 of a 247-
page book. This is roughly equivalent to Ellery Queen issu-
ing his Challenge to the Viewer immediately following the
opening credits!

Keeler's complicated tales of predestination may be
founded on an Eastern-mystical philosophy, but their action
is carried out in a very un-mystical milieu. Keeler loves
America--especially Chicago. He loves things new and
strange--especially novel inventions (most of which he made
up himself) and obscure facts about little-known subjects

(many of which he also made up). He loves the freakish and
the slightly seamy--especially the lore of the carnival and
the intricacies of modern slang. His stories always seem to
take place just this side of the tracks, where the upstand-
ing still have ample opportunity to brush shoulders with the
gangsters, freaks and grifters of a less savory but much
more romantic and exciting world. The heroes in both these
books have a touch of the other side to them: they are quick
but excitable, honorable but hard-boiled, and even if they
never engage in any physical violence they seem perfectly
willing to bust noses if necessary.

The language of the narrative is their language . . .
and like everything else, it's peculiarly Keelerian. Everyone speaks a strange mixture of street slang and thesaurian
jaw-breakers, delivered as if the speaker is nearly out of
breath, well-larded with pauses, dashes and exclamation
marks. The speakers of this odd patois can't bear to leave
out a single detail. Their sentences are like midget Keeler
novels, full of clauses and qualifications, of irrelevant
details and interjected clarifications. In Keelerworld,
even newspapers dote on detail: a brief report on a train
wreck describes the contents of a traveling case found
amidst the wreckage all the way down to an amber-handled
razor and a pair of purple pajamas emblazoned with yellow
circles! The frenetic language of Keelerese soon becomes
addictive, and reading several Keelers in a row is guaran-
teed to have a definite effect on your writing style. But
this peculiar HSK lingo is simply another ingredient which,
when combined with all the other components of the novel,
helps create the unique Keeler character.

That unique character is the main attraction of a Keeler novel anyway, not the puzzle to be solved. Certainly
there are questions to be answered, but not questions of the
"whodunit?" type. The questions are "How does this fit?"
and "How will he ever get out of this one?" Neither can
Keeler claim many of the virtues usually demanded of a "good
mystery writer." His characters are usually pure cardboard;
what motivations and actions they manifest are only for the
benefit of the plot. It is not suspense which keeps the
reader turning the pages asking, "What happens now?" It is
rather the fascination of the audience of a conjuring act.
The reader reads breathlessly on, wondering "How in the
world can he ever top this?"

The main attraction of Keeler is his technique. His
artifice is his art, and vice versa. The reader finds himself constantly marvelling at the clever dovetailing of the
pieces, smiling in admiration when a particularly outlandish
bit of business drops neatly into place, howling in glee
when the last-page switcheroo deftly answers the final questions, twists the whole magilla around 180 degrees, and
yields a hitherto undreamed-of solution of supreme beauty.

This sort of appreciation is akin to the enjoyment of a
piece of music as the sum of a hundred parts blended into
one, or of a painting as innumerable strokes placed just
right so as to create a masterpiece. Perhaps this approach
limits Keeler's appeal to a certain type of reader. Certainly these differ greatly from the usual grounds for appreciat-
ing a novel. Usually, the novel is viewed as an alternate

world in which the reader lives for the duration of the
story. With Keeler, the reader looks on from a slight dis-
tance, fully aware of his manipulation at the author's hands.
Possibly the average mystery reader, searching more for emotional involvement than for intellectual pleasure, would
eventually tire of such games. Indeed, this may be why HSK
was finally abandoned by American publishers and had to seek
European markets for his final works.
    Nevertheless, I would dearly like to see a paperback
renaissance of Keeler. With a bit of promotion, an enter-
prising publisher could climb on the series bandwagon with a
virtually inexhaustable supply of some of the craziest, most
appealing American mysteries ever written . . . and intro-
duce whole new generations of readers to the whacky world of
Harry Stephen Keeler.

[*The Riddle of the Traveling Skull*: Dutton, 1934. *The Skull
of the Waltzing Clown*, Dutton, 1935.
    Ron Harris is no stranger to *SSRS*; as this publica-
tion's art director, he has contributed covers and interior
illos, and of course the great Shot Scott comic strip. Ron
works in Palo Alto as a free-lance artist and what-have-you.
He also played Inspector Richard Queen to my Ellery in an
early production of the Num Nume Theatré of the Air! A.S.]

Art takes a brief look at *The Wonderful Scheme of Mr. Christopher Thorne*, Dutton, 1936.
    This is the third and concluding volume of the massive,
messhuga Marceau Meganovel, the first two volumes being *The
Marceau Case* and *X. Jones of Scotland Yard*. Unlike those
first two books, which were collections of documents and
photos, this is a "straightforward" narrative--(the neces-
sity of quotation marks when applying that adjective to Keeler ought to be obvious by now). Its connection to the other
two volumes, in which, you may recall, the bizarre murder of
cosmetics magnate Andre Marceu was solved and solved again,
differently, is tenuous; all the lines of connection not
emerging until--as you might have guessed--the very last
chapter.
    Thorne is concerned with a typical Keeler hero, Phillip
Erskine, equipped with typical Keelerian lady friend, Alicia
Thorne, caught in a mind-bending web of distressing circumstance. Thorne, a Chicago moneylender, cooks up the scheme
noted in the title in order to rid himself of an annoying
Bible-quoting clerk in his office, a strange lad of mixed
origins with the picturesque name of Ebenezer Sitting-Down-
Bear. In addition, Thorne's scheme has the object of rid-
dding his househole of Erskine, whose attentions toward
Thorne's adopted daughter are not appreciated.
    The "caper" which Thorne cooks up, and which Keeler de-
scribes in loving detail, is a preposterous web of jiggery-
pokery involving a fake rare book, a cunningly crafted bag-
with-false-bottom (made by one Hans Kalbringer, whose dialect would have tickled Milt Gross, and whose skills might
have been useful to John Barr of *Travelling Skull*, another
specialist in exotic luggage), stolen money, trips to New
Orleans, passage on the Amazonian Queen, and Lord knows what
else.

There is also the inevitable Chinese element, this time
in the person of Erskine's adoptive father, Daddy Quong, who
quotes Kong Fu Tse and lectures upon the working of the Law
of Karma at the drop of a hat. Daddy Quong, it seems is
tied into the Marceau web by virtue of his having been swin-
dled years ago by one Oliver Edward Marceau, the black sheep
American member of the Marceau family.

All ends happily, with the help of innumerable Keeler
coincidences, the Mardi Gras, the machinations of a con man
named Cantrell, and, at the wrap up, the publication of Xen-
ius Jones' solution to the Marceau murder. Light is shed
upon the origins of Andre Marceau's midgetphobia; the where-
abouts of O.E. Marceau; how to get gas, oil and water from
three plants to three houses whithout crossing lines; and
assorted other loose ends. Absolutely dumbfounding.

Rich Morrissey takes a look at *The Riddle of the Yellow Zuri*.

From Art's description, I knew that Harry Stephen Keeler's works were full of bizarre devices and improbable coincidences. But when Art sent me a copy of *The Riddle of the
Yellow Zuri* I found out that, strange though it seems, he
actually has the ability to make those devices and coincidences seem *believable*! By carefully starting out gradually,
testing the reader's suspension of disbelief at each stage
and keeping the most incredible elements hidden from the
reader and the protagonist until he's set the stage for them,
Keeler just barely manages to slip under the wire as a "mystery" writer--even though, as Art said, only a madman would
ever be able to deduce Keeler's intricate sequences of
events from the few clues that are given.

Yellow Zuri's protagonist, a young investigator for the
United States Government of false mining claims, is offered
$250 for acting as agent to a greasy stranger who's looking
for a lost snake--the exact reason is as obscure to him as
it is to the reader. The story moves fast after that, with
a mysterious bequest from his missing adoptive father and
future father-in-law arriving out of the blue barely in time
to save the hero's wayward brother-in-law from disgrace. By
the time a bit of clever detective work and a good deal of
fantastic luck have revealed the true nature of the bequest
and the real reason the stranger wanted the snake, the protagonist, and, along with him, the reader--who even a few
pages before would have considered such a thing, in Keeler's
own words, a coincidence that could "occur only in the minds
of fevered writers of fiction"--is ready to accept that bequest as a misinterpretation occasioned by an unfortunate
acrostic. After that, like the proverbial snowball rolling
downhill, the unexpected revelations come thick and fast in
the last few pages--finally straining even my credulity a
trifle as one very important and long-sought individual pops
up (in *drag*, yet!) in the very last paragraph. But by then,
Keeler's tied everything into such a neat knot that all I
can do is applaud . . . .

Especially as, every so often, he gently reminds us not
to take him too seriously. Surely the stereotypes of blacks,
Orientals and uneducated hillbillies with which *The Riddle
of the Yellow Zuri* abounds were outdated even in 1948 (the
book seems to be dated around then--though there's no copy-

right date, so I can't be sure [Rich' guess is a bit off;
the book dates from 1930!--A.S.])--I suppose the NAACP and
the like would be offended, but I found myself laughing in
spite of myself. In fact, the book reminds me of nothing so
much as the old serials and thrillers featuring hard-boiled
detectives and the like, with their exotic locales, plot-
advancing coincidences, and even comic relief raised to the
nth degree. Yes, Keeler had his own way of writing a "mystery" novel--but, strange though it may seem, it actually
worked for him!

[*The Riddle of the Yellow Zuri*: Dutton, 1931. British title:
The Tiger Snake: Ward, Lock, 1931.
     Rich is a comics and mystery fan from Massachusetts,
though his review was mailed from the "Chicago of the East,"
i.e., London! Rich is preparing to be a lawyer, and one
would hope he wouldn't take as gospel Keeler's views on
courtroom procedure, as portrayed in *The Amazing Web*! A.S.]

Art examines *Sing Sing Nights*. 1928.
     The reason why I chose to read this particular Keeler
at this time will become clear in a bit, but to proceed. . .
Like *Five Silver Buddhas*, this is another collection of Keeler's magazine pieces worked into a novel. Unlike *Buddhas*,
the framing story is less elaborate, consisting merely of
three men on death row telling three stories. The teller of
the best tale, as judged by the Irish jailer ("'Tis Shanahan
w'at has rid ahl th' magazines an' buks he c'n get his hands
ferninst."), gets a pardon, for complex reasons quite Keelerian. The condemned are all conveniently authors, whose
works sound suspiciously like books Keeler might have written.
     "The Strange Adventure of the Giant Moth" is the first
tale, and it is every bit a Keeler novel in miniature. Hero
Wilk Casperson, just on the verge of success with career and
lady friend, suddenly finds himself accused of jewel theft
and murder, through the workings of Keeler fate and the doings of: Moonface Eddie Chang, thief; Cecil Gryce a.k.a.
Wellington Cawthorne, con man; Professor Aloysius Silvester,
expert on moths; *Vergitilla Phyleas*, giant Central American
moth; Ushi Yatsura, Japanese; and several others. The device
of the "unfortunate acrostic," mentioned by Rich in connection with *Yellow Zuri*, gets an early tryout in this tale.
     The second tale, "The Strange Adventure of the Twelve
Coins of Confucius," has to do with the efforts of Jason Barton, bright young reporter for the *Chicago Evening Dispatch*,
to secure an interview with Princess O Lyra Seng; if he
fails, he loses his job. He gets the interview, but in the
process becomes involved in the search for the coins in the
title, through the convenient murder of a laundryman named
Sam Toy. This is another Keeler-in-miniature (with struc-
tural similarities to *The Face of the Man from Saturn*), in
which characters are not all they seem to be, in which every
event ties in to every other, in which hero gets success and
girl at the end.
     The final tale, "The Strange Adventure of the Missing
Link," is much shorter than the other two, and less Keller-
ian. It's rather like an O. Henry story, had O. Henry

turned to writing about brain transplants from man to goril-
la and back again! The final tale concluded, the workings
of the Keeler web come into play again to resolve the problem facing the taletellers; who, incidentally, paused between tales to discuss, in mathematical shorthand, the
theory of plot building according to precepts no doubt laid
down in *Mechanics and Kinematics of Web-Work Plot Construction* by G. Who?

And finally . . . KEELER ON THE SCREEN!
   If I had any lingering doubts that the Law of Cross and
Re-Cross was in fact operational, they were dispelled when a
local TV station chose to run a certain film just in time
for a review to be included in this Keeler section. That
film was a 1935 Monogram production, "The Mysterious Mr.
Wong," one of apparently three movies made from Keeler's
stories. This one was "Suggested by 'The Twelve Coins of
Confucius,'" discussed directly above.
   As is implied by "suggested," the story and the movie
are only similar in spots. One would be dreaming if one
were to expect Keeler's eccentric approach to storytelling
to be translated to the screen intact. The major points of
similarity are: the hero is a newshound named Jason Barton;
the coins are the MacGuffin; some small bits of business
carry over--the murder of Sam Toy, the clue of the laundry
ticket, the hiding place of the coins. Beyond that, it's
all Monogram's story. Barton's romance with the Princess
disapperas, along with the Princess; the love interest instead provided by the switchboard girl at the paper. The
HSK jigsaw plotting is nowhere in evidence, replaced by
ordinary linear melodrama.
   It's a fun movie, though, but hardly great film art--as
one would be bound to expect from Monogram, it's a typical
B-grade quicky. Reliable Wallace Ford plays Barton in the
Lee Tracy fashion, and I imagine Keeler would have enjoyed
his wisecracking, slangy dialogue: "He's no pushover; he's
a slick lug. He works with a knife and he's never out of
work!" Arline Judge plays his girlfirend, Fred Warren plays
the Irish cop on the Chinatown beat, Lotus Long adds exotic
color as Mr. Wong's daughter. William Nigh directed.
   Oh yes, Mr. Wong. Mr. Wong, a character nowhere in
evidence in the Keeler story, is an evil mastermind determined to collect the coins of Confucius. He masquerades as
an old shopkeeper, slinks through secret panels, sends shuf-
fling hatchetmen on missions of murder, happily applies red-
hot irons to the humble persons of those opposing his plans
for conquest in his back room torture chamber. Who plays
Mr. Wong? Why, Bela Lugosi! Who else? Bela Lugois's attempts to strain a Chinese dialect through his thick "I
never drink . . . wine!" Hungarian accent have to be heard
to be believed. Suffice to say that his approach to dialect
is every bit as bizarre as anything Keeler ever pulled off
on the printed page!
   It should be noted, to dispel confusion, that the Mr.
Wong character portrayed by Lugosi in this film is no relation to the Mr. Wong, detective, portrayed by his old horror
flic confrere Boris Karloff in a half-dozen films, also by
Monogram. All of which suggests a curtain line known to

anyone who's seen *What's Up Tiger Lily*, but I can't quite
bring myself to use it!

That about concludes this issue's sojourn into the alternate universe of Keelerland. My thanks to all concerned.
I might as well fill this space by quoting that section
of *Sing Sing Nights* already mentioned, in which Keeler sets
forth his notions of plot construction (Mike Nevins has provided a handy condensation, which should just about fit, I
hope!):

> The author . . . must first get clear in his
> mind that, in that web we call a plot, any charac-
> ter or vital inanimate object such as a letter, or
> a weapon, or a photograph, will constitute a
> thread. He must therefore first conceive of a
> thread which we may call the view-point thread, or
> thread representing the eyes of the character
> through whom most of the story is to be seen, and
> which we may term thread "A". This thread "A"
> must figure with another thread "B: in an opening
> incident which we will term incident "n", since
> its chronological order relative to the very ear-
> liest incident in the entire plot structure de-
> pends solely upon what revelations shall subse-
> quently be made as to vital happenings occurring
> prior to the actual opening of the story. . . .
> After inventing incident "n" between thread "A"
> and thread "B", there must be invented immediately
> an incident of numerical order "n+1", involving
> threat "A" with still another thread "C"; then an
> incident "n+2+ involving the same thread "A" with
> one "D"; then an incident "n+3" comprising an in-
> cident between threat "A" and a still further
> thread "E"; and this, to avoid an impasse, must
> be carried on as a rule to not less than an inci-
> dent of order "n+5"; and now mark well the essen-
> tial desideratum of this preliminary invention.
> Here it is: incident "n" must produce incident
> "n+1"; "n+2" must be the result of incident "n+1";
> "n+3" must be the result of "n+2"; and so on.
> This much correctly done, any writer--no matter
> who he be--will have a real set of threads with
> which to weave, as well as the nucleus--if we may
> use such a term--of the web itself.

In short, Harry Stephen Keeler!

THE NERO WOLFE SAGA
PART II
BY GUY M TOWNSEND

["Before I Die" [October 1946], published in *Trouble in Triplicate*, 1949.]

The next episode of the Saga is "Before I Die" [October 1946], a novella which was published in *Trouble in Triplicate* in 1949. This one is pretty light fare, but entertaining for all that. The time is during the "Great Meat Shortage," and Wolfe, for whom Archie tells us "a meal without a meat was an insult," is suffering grievously. So it is that when Wolfe is approached by gangster Dazy Perrett, "King of the Black Market," to do a job for him, Wolfe overcomes his normal reluctance to associate with such disreputable characters and agrees to see him with an eye towards utilizing the gangster's underworld connections to get some black market meat. Alas, our hero has feet of clay: "I am on the whole a respectable and virtuous citizen, but like everyone else I have my smudges. Where is some meat?"

What Dazy wants Wolfe to do is the weakest part of the story. He has a daughter who he does not want to know is his daughter. When rival gangsters discover that he has a daughter (but not who the daughter is), Dazy brings in a ringer to impersonate the real daughter. The ringer then proceeds to blackmail Dazy, and Dazy appeals to Wolfe to stop her from blackmailing him and also to stop Dazy's real daughter from using a mannerism which is likely to identify her to Dazy's rivals as his daughter. I said it was weak, didn't I? Well, from this situation arises a series of murders and lead-slinging which would not be much out of place in Hammett's *Red Harvest*, one of the beg shoot-outs occuring in Wolfe's office and another on his front stoop. This amount of violence is unusual in these tales, but then Wolfe does not usually associate with the likes of Dazy Perrett. The murderer is obvious before the story is half finished, and the reader who is surprised when Wolfe finally unmasks him (or her) should be forced to read a year's run of the Dick Tracy comic strip (that's cruel and inhuman punishment, I know, but this is *really* obvious).

A good many familiar characters make appearances in this tale, including Cramer, Theodore, Saul and Fritz. And Rowcliff, of whom Archie remarks, "Lieutenant Rowcliff of Homicide was one of the reasons why I doubted if the world would ever reach the point of universal brotherhood. It didn't seem feasible as long as opinions were still loose like mine of Rowcliff." Incidentally, Rowcliff takes Archie downtown in this tale.

We are given another example of Wolfe's distaste for crude language: "Violet [the pseudo-daughter] let out a word. Ordinarily I try to report conversations without editing but we'll let that one go. Wolfe made a face. He never cares for coarse talk, but he can stand it better from men than from women." And "Before I Die" also gives us the first instance of Wolfe fleeing the room because a woman is crying:

"'Good God,' Wolfe muttered in a tone of horror, and got to his feet and went."

Wolfe's yellow pajamas are again in evidence, and a new element of his bedroom apparel is introduced--yellow slippers with turned-up toes. And Archie tells us with some distaste that the telephone in Wolfe's room is also yellow. Bright yellow, in fact.

There are a few physical developments of note in "Before I Die." Archie remarks that the brownstone is "not far from North River." More to the point, he gives a woman detailed instructions on how to get to the house from the rear: "From Thirty-fourth Street and Eleventh Avenue go east on Thirty-fourth Street. It's ninety-two paces for me, so it will be about a hundred and twenty for you. At that point there is a narrow passage between two buildings--a loading platform on the left of it and a wholesale paper products place on the right. Go in along the passageway and I'll met you at the far end of it and let you in at our back door." Would some New Yorker out there follow these directions and let me know what happens? We are also informed, for the first time I believe, that at the back of the brownstone is "our little private yard where Fritz grows chives and tarragon and other vegetation."

Entering the brownstone now, we are given some new information about the south room, which is on the same floor as Archie's room: "On various occasions all kinds had slept in it, from a Secretary of State to a woman who had poisoned three husbands and was making a fourth one very sick." Going downstairs, we learn that both doors to the front room are soundproofed, and that the couch in the office is placed in "the corner made by the wall of the lavatory that had been built in." We learn, thus, not only the placement of the couch, but also that the lavatory was not a part of the office when the house was originally built.

And just a few items for the *Odds and Ends* section: Archie has been with Wolfe "for over ten years;" Wolfe shuts Archie out briefly on this case; Archie says, "I never bothered with the elevator;" and Archie makes a date with a girl to have dinner at Ribeiro's, the first (and perhaps only) time that restaurant is mentioned in the Saga.

[*Too Many Women* [March-April 1947], published in 1947.]

Too Many Women was published in 1947. Wolfe is deep into one of his lazy spells and Archie has to badger and manipulate to get him to undertake the job he is being offered by Jasper Pine, president of Naylor-Kerr, Inc., manufacturers of engineers' equipment and supplies. Some months earlier one of Naylor-Kerr's employees, one Waldo Moore by name, was killed in an apparent hit-and-run accident. The police were content to leave it at that, but one of Naylor-Kerr's employees is promoting the idea that it was deliberate murder, and Jasper Pine, as president of the company, wants Wolfe to determine whether it was in fact murder. Note that the commission, which Wolfe eventually accepts, is not to discover who the murderer is, but only if there is a murderer. Another murder soon makes it clear that Moore *was* murdered, and Wolfe then undertakes to expose the murderer's identity. By book's end the reader is not likely to be sur-

prised at the identity of the murderer, but it's still a
pleasant read.

Too Many Women just bulges with Saga developments,
though not too many of them relate to Wolfe. We learn that
he now weighs 340 pounds, which is a sizeable jump from his
last reported weight, and first mention is made of his practice of reading three books at once. He still persists in
the barbarism of dog-earing his books. Archie makes a few
statements about his boss which are of some interest: "His
murmur is Wolfe at his worst;" "I won't go so far as to say
that he never liked women, but he sure didn't like women who
picked up the ball and started off with it;" "when he does-
n't close his eyes while I am making a report it usually
means that part of his mind is on something else, and I never know how big a part;" "There was no joing about food with
him."

Of himself, Archie says that he is "the heart, liver,
lung, and gizzard of the private detective business of Nero
Wolfe, Wolfe being merely the brains." Of his relationship
with Wolfe, Archie remarks that "a coolness had sprung up
between Wolfe and me. These coolnesses averaged about four
a week, say, a couple of hundred a year. This particular
one had two separate aspects: first, my natural desire for
him to buy a new car opposed to his pigheaded determination
to wait another year; and second, his notion of buying a
noiseless typewriter opposed to my liking for the one we
had." Wolfe is also at odds with Fritz over the question of
putting sweet basil in clam chowder (Fritz is against it)
and with Theodore over the introduction of some begonias
into the plant room (Theodore being an orchid snob). Theodore, incidentally, now lives in the brownstone (where is
his room located?). Archie now supplies *another* reason why
Wolfe sometimes shuts him out of some aspects of some cases:
"His stated reason was that I worked better if I thought it
all depended on me. His actual reason was that he loved to
have a curtain go up revealing him balancing a live seal on
his nose."

Actually, we learn a great deal about Archie on this
outing. His salary is $200 per week (and remember, he gets
room and board for nothing), which is extremely good for the
mid-forties. He is one hell of a fighter, as he demon-
strates when picked on by a fellow several sizes larger than
himself. He has an "arsenal" consisting of two revolvers
and an automatic. The automatic is a Wembly; further speci-
fics not available on either of the revolvers. Doorbell answering has devinitely become his job now, and his drink is
bourbon in this novel. Of his extra-curricular activities
Archie tells us, "Saturday night I usually take some person
of an interesting sex to a hockey or basketball game." He
tells a woman that he is half gypsy, to which flummery she
responds by providing us with considerable detail about
Archie's background: his father, who is still alive, is
named James Abner Goodwin, and his mother's maiden name was
Leslie; he has two brothers and two sisters; and he was born
in Canton, Ohio, in 1914, and so is 33 at the time of this
tale.

Just about every regular character in the Saga shows up
in this one: Lily Rowan is mentioned, but doesn't put in an

appearance; Purley Stebbins, Archie's "favorite sergeant," is around, together with Rowcliff and Cramer. Cramer goes so far as to accuse Wolfe of covering for the murderer, and of Rocliff Archie says "his opinion of me is a perfect match for mine of him. Durkin, Cure, Cather and Keems are all called in, as is Saul, about whom Archie says some nice things: he had "the best pair of eyes I know of, not even excepting Wolfe;" he "was the best free-lance operative in New York. He was the only colleague I knew that I would give a blank check to and forget it." Archie also says, "Saul never swore," right after Saul says, "Damn the luck." Lon Cohen puts in an appearance via the telephone, as usual, and Archie says of him that "he knew more facts than the Police Department and the Public Library combined." We also learn something new about Fritz: "In his French-Swiss way he can be a very tenacious kidder."

We finally learn something more about Rusterman's—"It was the best grub in New York outside of Wolfe's own dining room. . . . The booths along the left wall upstairs . . . were so well partitioned that they were practically private rooms. . . . Rusterman's was owned and bossed by Wolfe's old friend, Marko Vukcic."

There are a few physical developments as well. We learn for the first time that the check writing table is made of massaranduba. The clear glass window in the front door is said to have been recently replaced by a one-way glass panel. And the address is now given as 914 West 35th Street.

There is an oddity in the story which may be a typo in my edition (DBC): Archie tries to set up an appointment with Wolfe for *5:00* p.m., which is right in the middle of Wolfe's 4:00-6:00 session in the plant rooms.

Finally, beef steak is 90¢ a pound, higher that I would have expected for that period.

["Man Alive" [June 1947], published in *Three Doors to Death*, 1950.]

"Man Alive" was published in *Three Doors to Death* in 1950. Paul Nieder and Jean Daumery were partners in the firm of Daumery and Nieder, clothing designers and manufacturers. Paul Nieder was in love with his partner's wife, Helen, and shortly after her death in a riding accident Nieder committed suicide by jumping naked into a geyser in Yellowstone Park. Some six weeks prior to the time our people become involved, Daumery is drowned in a boating accident.

Nero Wolfe and company are drawn in when Paul Nieder's niece Cynthia comes to the office, acquaints them with the above story, then declares that she has seen her uncle alive in New York a week before. She hires Wolfe (with a $2,000 retainer) to find Uncle Paul, but before anything can be done Uncle Paul's body shows up dead in the offices of Daumery and Nieder, and Cynthia is the prime suspect. Wolfe frees her from suspicion by revealing the real murderer's identity in a workmanlike fashion. A good short mystery, but not one of Stout's best.

It does, however, have several Saga developments of note. We are given yet another description of Wolfe's finger twirling habit, with yet another motivation behind it:

"He leaned back, shut his eyes, and began making little cir- cles on the arm of his chair with the tip of his forefinger. He was flummoxed good, his nose pushed right in level with his face." We are also given more information on Wolfe and women: "He couldn't stand emphatic women;" and "the only thing that shakes Wolfe as profoundly as having a mean in- terrupted is a bawling woman. His reaction to the first is rage, to the second panic." Wolfe's largely mercenary in- terest in solving murders is pointed up by Archie's comment that "to get any attention from Wolfe a murder must be at- tached to a client with money to spend and a reason for spending it." There are also a few other items of interest regarding Wolfe. He speaks of a "habeas corpus ad subjicien- dum," which is the first "big word" (of sorts) we've en- countered in a while, and Archie remarks that "Wolfe heaved a sigh that filled his whole interior," which is sort of like digging half a hole. And finally, Archie tells us that this case was one occasion when "Wolfe outsmarted him- self. Not far from the top of the list of the things he abhors is being a witness at a trial, and ordinarily he takes good care to handle things so that he won't get a subpoena. But only last week I had the pleasure of sitting in the courtroom and watching him--and listening to him--in the witness chair."

Of Archie himself he tells us "I am just under six feet and weigh a hundred and eighty," and on one occasion he says "he don't," but that's about it for this tale.

The other regulars are rather scarce in this one. Cramer, of course, is present, behaving in a very boorish and discourteous fashion, even going so far as to force his way into the house past Fritz and interrupt Wolfe at his lunch. Regarding Cramer's cigars Archie says "he never lit one but only chewed it." Stebbins is barely present and is referred to by Archie as "my favorite Sergeant." Saul Pan- zer, "the best free-lance operative on earth," makes a brief appearance, while Lily Rowan is mentioned in passing. And I seem to recall an earlier appearance by this next fellow-- Archie and Saul take "a taxi driven by our old pal Herb Aron- son, whom we often used."

There is a fair amount of physical information in this episode. It is a ten minute walk from the brownstone to 496 Seventh Avenue, which is another hint a New York fan might follow up. (Also, Archie repeats his remark that the brownstone is "not far from the river.") The dining room, we are told, is "across the hall from the office," the doors and walls of the front room are again said to be soundproof, and the one-way glass panel in the front door is still being used. We are also given a hint as to how the office furni- ture is arranged. Archie says, "my desk . . . is so placed that a half-turn of my swivel chair puts me facing Wolfe, and with another half-turn I am confronting the red leather chair beyond the end of his desk where a lone visitor is usually seated."

And at the time of this tale Wolfe has just bought a new Cadillac sedan, which makes it more or less Archie's since, as he remarks, he is the only one of the brownstone's four residents who knows how to drive. Actually, Fritz "knew how to drive but pretended he didn't, and had no license."

ODDS & ENDS ::: Wolfe's signal for beer is two short
buzzes, which is (I think) the first time this has been mentioned. The doorbell-answering situation is touched on
briefly: "During meals Fritz always answers the door." And
finally, Archie serves some guests a snack called mahallebi.
The closest I can come to this is the mahaleb, or the mahaleb cherry as it is sometimes called. I'm inclined to doubt
that this is what Archie was serving, however, since, while
the mahaleb is used to make a cordial, it is not a very pre-
possessing fruit on its own.

[*And Be a Villain* [March-April 1948], published in 1948.]
        And Be a Villain was published in 1948. Madeline Fras-
er has a fantastically successful radio talk show, one of
the sponsors of which is Hi-Spot, The Drink You Dream Of.
During one of her broadcasts a guest, the publisher of an
outrageously expensive horse-racing sheet, takes a drink
from his glass (which is supposed to contain Hi-Spot) and
keels over dead from cyanide poisoning.
        Because it is incometax time, and because Wolfe has
just written a large check to a "World government outfit,"
the coffers are rather low. So low, in fact, that Wolfe
overcomes his laziness and casts about for a profitable job,
settling at last on the above murder. He has Archie go to
Miss Fraser and company and offer to discover the murderer
for $20,000 plus expenses. If he doesn't catch the murderer
he gets only his expenses. "Wolfe almost never takes a case
on a contingent basis, but when he needs money he breaks
rules, especially his own." The case is a difficult and
complex one, and before it is over the murderer claims two
more victims, one by the rather pedestrian method of a gun
shot to the head, the other in a much more ingenious fashion.
Needless to say, Wolfe collects his expenses *and* the $20,000.
        And Be a Villain is a highly significant episode in the
Saga, because in it we are first acquainted with Wolfe's
bete noire, Arnold Zeck. Zeck is Wolfe's Professor Moriarty,
only more evil and more powerful than the late and unlament-
ed mathematician. In investigating the case at Hand Wolfe
has uncovered a vast blackmail network in which Zeck has a
hand, and Zeck calls him and warns him off. We learn that
this is the third time Zeck has spoken to Wolfe on the phone,
the first being on 9 June 1943 and the second on 16 January
1946, on both of which earlier occasions he also warned
Wolfe off. Zeck: "I was pleased to see that you did limit
your efforts as I suggested. That showed--" Wolfe breaks
in: "I limited them because no extension of them was required to finish the job I was hired for. I did not limit
them because you suggested it, Mr. Zeck." Zeck was annoyed
that Wolfe knew his name, and Archie was surprised to know
that Wolfe knew it: "How did that happen?" Wolfe: "Two
years ago I engaged some of Mr. Bascom's men without telling
you. He sounded as if he were a man of resource and resolution, and I didn't want to get you involved." Wolfe orders
Archie to forget that he knows Zeck's name. Wolfe himself
shows us the extent of his respect (in the sense that one
respects a tiger or a cobra) for Zeck when he says to Archie:
"I'll tell you this. If ever, in the course of my business,

I find that I am committed against him and must destroy him,
I shall leave this house, find a place where I can work--and
sleep and eat if there is time for it--and stay there until
I have finished. I don't want to do that, and therefore I
hope I'll never have to." Naturally, Archie disregards
Wolfe's instructions to forget about Zeck, and the first opportunity he has he pumps Lon Cohen for information on him.
Lon tells him, "Zeck is a question mark. I've heard that he
owns twenty assemblymen and six district leaders, and I've
also heard that he is merely a dried fish. There's a rumor
that if you print something about him that he resents your
body is washed ashore at Montauk Point, mangled by sharks,
but you know how the boys talk. One little detail . . . .
There's not a word on him in our morgue. I had occasion to
look once, several years ago--when he gave his yacht to the
Navy. Not a thing, which is peculiar for a guy that gives
away and owns the highest hill in Westchester." When Wolfe
gets the case all cleared up Zeck calls back to congratulate
Wolfe "on keeping your investigation within the limits I
prescribed. That has increased my admiration of you." "'I
like to be admired,' Wolfe said curtly. 'But when I undertake an investigation I permit prescription of limits only
by the requirements of the job. If that job had taken me
across your path you would have found me there.'" When
Archie suggests that the day may yet come when Wolfe will
have to deal with Zeck, Wolfe replies, "It may. I hope not."
      Beside the Zeck element, there are numerous other de-
velopments relevant to the Saga, a large number of which
deal directly with Wolfe. In fact, it is rather an embar-
rassment of riches. Archie tells us that it is Wolfe's
"conviction that all women alive are either extremely dan-
gerous or extremely dumb." And while we're on the subject
of women and Wolfe we might take note of Archie's remark
that "the one thing that scares Wolfe out of his senses is
a woman in a tantrum." Regarding Wolfe's reputation for
never leaving the house, Archie is asked, "Is that just a
publicity trick or does he really like it?" To which he replies, "I guess both. He's very lazy, and he's scared to
death of moving objects, especially things on wheels." We
are given a good bit about Wolfe's habits, likes, dislikes
and such: his aversion to the use of contact as a verb is
mentioned; "he never eats between dinner and breakfast;"
"Wolfe seldom takes on beer during the hour preceding dinner;" "he never rises when men enter, and his customary
routine when a woman enters is to explain, if he feels like
taking the trouble, that he keeps his chair because getting
out of it and back in again is a more serious undertaking
for him than for most men;" "the tip of his right forefinger
was doing a little circle on the arm of his chair, around
and around," and this time it means he is thinking; he
"tucked his napkin in the V of his vest;" he doesn't like
geraniums; he always has his breakfast on a tray in his bedroom (while Archie always has his "in the kitchen with
Fritz"). Archie remarks, "when I saw his lips pushing out,
and in again, and out and in, I knew he was exerting himself
to the limit," and he says that when Wolfe is in one of
these states of intense concentration "I can bang the typewriter or make phone calls or use the vacuum cleaner and he

doesn't hear it." Archie also comments on Wolfe's movements:
"I guess it's partly his size, unquestionably impressive,
which holds people's attention when he is in motion, but his
manner and style have a lot to do with it. You get both suspense and surprise. You know he's going to be clumsy and
wait to see it, but by gum you never do. First thing you
know there he is, in his chair or wherever he was bound for,
and there was nothing clumsy about it at all. It was smooth
and balanced and efficient." Still, Wolfe is a heavy man,
and "during his first ten minutes in a chair minor adjust-
ments are always required." A couple of more items: Wolfe
flexes his long dormant vocabulary a time or two, producing
dysgenic and temerarious; and Archie mentions that he is
wearing a yellow shirt, which is, I think, the first time
that the color of Wolfe's clothing (except his p.j.s) has
been mentioned.

This time Wolfe trys to take the easy way out, giving
every item of information that he has to Cramer in return
for a promise that if this information enables the police to
catch the murderer Cramer will so advise Wolfe's clients.
This infuriates Archie--"to me it was only too evident that
Wolfe had really done a strip act, to avoid overworking his
brain." "It was not," Archie tells us, "properly speaking,
a relapse. Relapse is my word for it when he gets so offended or disgusted by something about a case, or so appalled by
the kind or amount of work it is going to take to solve it,
that he decides to pretend he has never heard of it, and re-
jects it as a topic of conversation. This wasn't like that.
He just didn't intend to work unless he had to." To get
Wolfe to get off his can and back to work Archie has Lon
Cohen arrange an editorial in the *Gazette* critical of
Wolfe's inaction. In fact, Archie gets so annoyed at Wolfe
that he tells him he quits. Wolfe replies, "Some day there
will be a crisis. Either you'll get insufferable and I'll
fire you, or I'll get insufferable and you'll quit. But
this isn't the day and you know it."

Saul Panzer is fairly active in this one, and Archie
has more invariably good things to say about him: "He is so
good that he demands, and gets, double the market, and any
day of the week he gets so many offers that he can pick as
he pleases. I have never known him to turn Wolfe down except when he was so tied up he couldn't shake loose." In
this episode he fails (through no fault of his own) to ac-
complish a mission which Wolfe assigned to him and he says,
"This is the third time I've flopped on you in ten years,
and that's too often. I don't want you to pay me, not even
expenses." Archie records Wolfe's reply thusly: "Nonsense.'
Wolfe never gets riled with Saul.' Archie also adds to our
physical description of Saul--"coming only up to the middle
of my ear, and of slight build."

Cramer, for whom Archie says "Mr. Bluff" is one of 15
aliases he has, is also described: "He was in fact getting
fairly gray and his middle, though it would never get into
Wolfe's class, was beginning to make pretensions, but his
eyes were as sharp as ever and his heavy broad shoulders
showed no inclination to sink under the load." Cramer and
Wolfe are unusually civil toward each other in this one, almost considerate, in fact, and Cramer even calls Archie by

his first name, thereby occasioning Archie to remark, "He called me Archie only when he wanted to peddle the impression that he regarded himself as one of the family, which he wasn't."

Marko Vukcic is mentioned, as "an old friend" of Wolfe's who "dropped in for a Sunday evening snack--five kinds of cheeze, guava jelly, freshly roasted chestnuts, and almond tarts." Archie says that he "manages" Rusterman's but does not say that he owns it.

And speaking of restaurants, Archie and Lon Cohen drop in at a place called Pietro's, which is the first time that eatery has been mentioned (and perhaps the last?).

Before getting to the physical Saga developments of this episode, we should note that Purley Stebbins, Lt. Rowcliff and Deputy Commissioner O'Hara all make brief appearances, and that Doc Vollmer is mentioned but does not appear. And lastly, we are told that Fritz "never goes to bed until after Wolfe does."

We are given a new address for the brownstone--918 West 35th Street--and, at last, a detailed description of the ground floor:

> There are four rooms on the bround floor of Wolfe's old brownstone house on West Thirty-fifth Street not far from the Hudson River. As you enter from the stoop, on your right are an enormous old oak clothes rack with a mirror, the elevator, the stairs, and the door to the dining room. On your left are the doors to the front room, which doesn't get used much, and to the office. The door to the kitchen is at the rear, the far end of the hall.

> The office is twice as big as any of the other rooms. It is actually our living room too, and since Wolfe spends most of his time there you have to allow him his rule regarding furniture and accessories: nothing enters it or stays in it that he doesn't enjoy looking at. He enjoys the contrast between the cherry of his desk and the cardato of his chair, made by Meyer. The bright yellow couch has to be cleaned every two months, but he likes bright yellow. The three-foot globe over by the bookshelves is too big for a room that size, but he likes to look at it. He loves a comfortable chair so much that he won't have any other kind in the place, though he never sits on any but his own.

We also learn an additional fact about Wolfe's bedroom: "Since Wolfe likes plenty of air at night but a good warm room at breakfast time it had been necessary, long ago, to install a contraption that would automatically close his window at 6:00 a.m. As a result the eight o'clock temperature permits him to have his tray on a table near the window without bothering to put on a dressing gown."

Two last items need to be mentioned before leaving this episode. The doorbell-answering arrangement seems to have blurred somewhat: "Sometimes Fritz answers it and sometimes me--usually me, when I'm home and not engaged on something that shouldn't be interrupted." And lastly, we are told

34

that there are only 19 bottles of a brandy called Remisier in the U.S. and Wolfe has them all stashed away in his cellar.

["Omit Flowers" [July 1948], published in *Three Doors to Death*, 1950.]

"Omit Flowers" was published in *Three Doors to Death* in 1950. Wolfe's friend Marko Vukcic, "one of the only three people who called him by his first name," asks Wolfe to help out Virgil Pompa, a former friend of Marko's who used to be a good cook before he prostituted his talents by going to work for a restaurant chain. Pompa is accused of murdering the husband of the woman who owns the chain of "Ambrosia" restaurants, but Marko is convinced of Pompa's innocence despite the weight of the evidence against him, and appeals to Wolfe on Pompa's behalf. Wolfe reluctantly agrees, but only as a favor to Marko, and, since Wolfe does not take money for doing favors for friends, he does not earn a fee when he solves this one. Before the investigation has a fair chance to get underway Mrs. Whitten, Pompa's boss and the wife of the murdered man, is herself the victim of an unsuccessful murderous attack, and Archie performs in a fashion which even Wolfe has to admit "was unquestionably brilliant." Wolfe's solution to the problem in this fast-paced and entertaining episode is a bit too pat, if the truth be told, but that's an easily overlooked flaw.

There are only a moderate number of Saga developments in "Omit Flowers." The story begins with Wolfe, Archie and Marko dining together "in one of the private rooms at Rusterman's," thus we find Wolfe outside of the brownstone for the first time in some while. Rusterman's, Archie tells us, "was the one place besides home where Wolfe really enjoyed eating." And we are further told that Marko not only runs it but owns it as well. While on the subject of Wolfe and eating we might remark here that Wolfe's practice of always breakfasting in his bedroom "on a tray brought by Fritz" is again mentioned. And it should also be noted that Marko dines in the brownstone one evening during the case. Archie endeavours to get Wolfe to leave the brownstone to interview Mrs. Whitten, who can hardly be expected to come to W. 35th St. immediately after being attacked, and Archie remarks to Marko that "it has been years . . . since I tried to get him to break his rule never to go anywhere outside his house on business, and I wouldn't waste breath on it now. But this has nothing to do with business. . . . This is for love, a favor to an old friend, which makes it entirely different. No question of rule-breaking is involved." As it happens, the need for leaving the house is almost immediately removed, as a result of which "Wolfe threw his head back and laughed. He did that about once a year." Wolfe does another quite unusual thing in this story: upon a woman entering the office he "got to his feet, and bowed, which was quite a tribute. . . . I've seen him react to a woman's entrance in that office with nothing but a ferocious scowl."

Of Archie we are given virtually no new information; his weight is still 180 pounds, but that's not news. Lon Cohen, Purley Stebbins, and Inspector Cramer all appear. Regarding the last mentioned, Archie says that "the man

about the chair" is a name he has used for years to tell
Wolfe that Cramer has arrived.

The front door receives a little attention. The one-
way glass panel is mentioned again, which brings up an interesting question--are such panels effective at night, when
the caller is standing in the dark and the hall within the
house is alight? The doorbell rings while Archie is occu-
pied in the office, and Archie says "under the circumstances
it was up to Fritz" to answer it. One last thing about the
door: "When I'm not in the house, especially at night, the
front door is always chain bolted, so I had to ring for
Fritz to let me in." Actually, there have been (and will
continue to be) many occasions when Archie has let himself
in with his key without bothering Fritz, so the "always" in
this statement is inaccurate.

ODDS & ENDS ::: The brownstone now has a television,
which apparently resides in the office. This is the first
mention of this machine in the Saga. Wolfe insists that one
of the people involved in the case, a woman, remain in the
brownstone overnight, and another woman stays with her.

I have neglected to mention the arrangement of the
plant rooms to this point, an oversight which I will have
to correct when I redo the Saga. For now it may be said
that both an "intermediate room" and a potting room are mentioned in this episode.

Finally, we are provided with a description of the second and third floors [first and second for the British and
European readers among us] of the brownstone: "Wolfe's room
is at the rear of the house on the second floor, which he
uses because its windows face south, and there is another
bedroom on that floor in front, unoccupied. On the third
floor my room is the one at the front, on the street, and
there is another spare at the rear which we call the South
Room," which is large and "has better furniture and rugs
[than the second floor spare], its own bathroom, and twin
bed."

["Door to Death" [December 1948], published in *Three Doors
to Death*, 1950.]

"Door to Death" was published in *Three Doors to Death*
in 1950. It is a most unusual short story in that all of it,
except for a brief closing chapter, takes place outside of
the brownstone, and in it Wolfe not only journeys with Archie 50 miles from New York by car, but he also performs the
unheard of feat of tramping across the countryside in the
dead of night, climbing up (and falling down) hills and
cliffs and even wading streams. And what is all of this
extraordinary behavior in aid of? Well, Theodore Horstman,
"tender and defender of the ten thousand orchids in the
plant rooms on the roof," has been called away indefinitely
by the illness of his mother, and Wolfe desperately needs to
find a replacement before the orchids suffer from neglect.
Andy Krasicki, who is currently gardening for Joseph G. Pitcairn up in Westchester County, is highly recommended by
Lewis Hewitt, and when phone calls and letters fail to coax
young Andy away from Pitcairn Wolfe resorts to the desperate
step of calling on the reluctant gardener in person. When
he sees Andy, however, he learns that the trip was unneces-

sary, since Andy had just written him a letter accepting the post. But before they can get away from the Pitcairn estate the body of Andy's fiancee of less than a day is discovered in the greenhouse, dead from being gassed with ciphogene when the greenhouse was fumigated the night before. Andy is locked up by the police, and Wolfe must find the real killer before they can get back to the brownstone and the ailing orchids. This is not accomplished, however, before Wolfe turns down a $100,000 bribe and meets up with some hostile authorities, most notably Lt. Con Noonan of the State Police, who "had been a stinker from the start, and it was only after the arrival of the D.A. [Cleveland Archer], who had good reason to remember the Fashalt case, that Wolfe and I had been accepted as human." The Fashalt case is not a recorded tale.

Saul is called in to help out. "As Wolfe had said, Fred or Orrie would do, but Saul Panzer was worth ten of them or nearly anyone else." We also learn that he is married, though I suspect this fact may have emerged earlier in the Saga.

Wolfe's weight is remarked on several times, Archie saying at one point that 300 pounds was an understatement and refering at another to Wolfe's 1/6 of a ton. Of his disinclination to go out Archie says, "He hates going outdoors and rarely does, and he would rather trust himself in a room alone with three or four mortal enemies than in a piece of machinery on wheels." Wolfe says a few quotable things in this one. On women--"Women do not require motives that are comprehensible by any intellectual process." And he speaks of "the inexorable miasma of murder," which is a bit much.

Lastly, he receives no fee for solfing this one, but he does get a gardener.

MYSTERY*FILE

Short Reviews by Steve Lewis

William Haggard, *Yesterday's Enemy* (Walker; c. 1976; first published in U.S.A., 1976; 204 pp.)

In this age of widespread technology and know-how, a bit of do-it-yourself nucleonics is quite possible and could easily blow up into a full-scale catastrophe. That's why Charles Russell, ex-head of the British Security Executive, is working so feverishly, hand-in-glove with a Russian general. His task, simple, but quite the reverse of the obvious. He must prove there's *nothing* behind the plot that could draw the great powers into an atomic confrontation. Even the appearance of such a plot could be spark enough.

Unfortunately there isn't any great sense of urgency involved, and the whole affair is undon with a most trivial solution. It's hard to get worked up over something as flimsy as this. (C minus)*

Brian Freeborn, *Good Luck Mister Cain* (St. Martin's; c. 1976; 134 pp.)

A small-time London con-man puts his neck on the line when he agrees, for ten thousand pounds, to take a step upward and become a hit-man against an IRA target. Since he's essentially non-political, the latter poses no problem, but to secure the job requires that he pose as Mr. Cain, a true killer at heart and unhappy at losing the job.

Lots of non-tourist description of London's lower sides, and told without compromise to the American ear. The result is a mildly interesting suspense tale viewed with considerable bemused detachment. (C plus)*

John Lutz, *Buyer Beware* (G. P. Putnam's Sons; c. 1976; 188pp.)

Private eyes tend to specialize these days. Alo Nudger, for example, comes highly recommended in child custody cases. That he's not the hard-boiled type is well illustrated by his dependence on antacid tablets, but enough money can overcome many qualms.

Murder is not in his line, but once persuaded, he takes his investigation into the efficient world of business and finance, which is faced with a deadly extension of the rules it plays by. Lutz has an eye for people and background that adds greatly to a tale that holds its own most of the way, yet I did wish the scheme were not ultimately so far-fetched, made all the more so by the rushed wrap-up. (C plus)*

Margaret Millar, *Ask for Me Tomorrow* (Random House; c. 1976; 179 pp.)

Gilly Decker's current husband is dying. In apparent fear of being left alone, she hires a young lawyer to head into Mexico to find her first husband. Hard upon his heels is a killer who seems determined to block off any chance of success.

---

* Reviews so marked have appeared earlier in the *Hartford Courant.*

Millar paints a not very complimentary view of life and legal justice in the land south of the border, and we are again forced to accept a California populated by its own brand of strange inhabitants found nowhere else. But it's a finely tuned, picturesque story with sharp convincing dialog, misfiring only slightly with an ending that just may result in more questions than it answers. (A minus)*

Sara Woods, *My Life Is Done* (St. Martin's; c. 1976; 223 pp.)
Barrister Antony Maitland is asked to investigate a case of blackmail--a stolen letter could embarrass a member of parliament who opposes a reservoir development in his home region.
There's little action. It's a classic case of parlor detection that still manages to result in two murders. Conversational nuances are cleverly used in the place of tangible evidence, but I suspect that many an armchair detective will feel disappointed with the degeneration into a courtroom confessional scene not unlike television's Perry Mason. (C plus)*

Donald Seaman, *The Terror Syndicate* (Coward, McCann & Geoghegan; c. 1976; 1st American edition, 1976; 214 pp.)
A novel about terrorist activities does not make for entertaining reading. Terrorism is a brutal business, and it reduces people to shells of living beings--the killers, the victims, and all too often the governments which must resort to an equal non-regard for life in their search for death-dealers.
Seaman's story chills but collapses halfway through. Professional agents become amateurs for the sake of the plot. Why else would they foolishly participate in an encounter group in dangerously unknown territory? A lot of killing and bloodshed, not too much suspense. (C)*

Heron Carvic, *Picture Miss Seeton* (Popular Library 00442; c. 1968; PL edition, February 1977; 176 pp.)
One big advantage in belonging to an organization like DAPA-EM, besides the opportunity to take part in several ongoing discussions of mysteries (among other things), is that other members are continually pointing out books and authors that you would have otherwise ignored or perhaps never even heard of. I was finally persuaded to give Dick Francis a try by sheer weight of numbers. In a recent mailing an article about Miss Seeton in Don Markstein's zine suggested that I was missing out on something else.
My affection for little old lady detectives carrying umbrellas previously began and ended with Miss Marple, but I'm sure that Miss Marple never wielded the brolly with Miss Seeton's assurance. Imagine interrupting a killer in an alleyway by jabbing him in the back to rebuke him for bad manners!
Trouble follows the little old innocent to her new cottage in the country. Gossipy neighbors somehow decide that she's involved with drug traffic and happily begin spreading their malicious rumors. Yet there's a grain of truth in their lies since quiet Plummergen has indeed become the center of operations for a gang of narcotics dealers, and Miss

Seeton's involvement is inevitable. She's situation-prone, you see. "My dear superintendent, if there were no such thing as coincidence, there would be no such word."

She thinks of herself as normal, but she has a certain psychic insight to look behind what she sees, and logical behavior in unusual circumstances can appear supremely idiocyncratic to others. Or more simply, somebody as nutty as this should not be missed. (A minus)

Christopher Bush, *The Case of the Counterfeit Colonel* (Macmillan; c. 1952; 240 pp.)

On page 176 is a challenge to the reader that can't be ignored, and I quote: "Too hard for you? Well, maybe it is, but it'll do you no harm to try to think it out." So in spite of some tough alibis and some quite unbelievable behavior on the part of Ludovic Travers' client, no, it wasn't too tough at all. Usually I'm the lazy kind of reader who is content to sit back and let the author do all the tedious work with timetables, fingerprints and such, but as I say, that's the kind of challenge that can't be turned down. In fact even though some of the details were off, in some ways I still like my version better.

The affair concerns a hunt for a missing wartime hero, a blackmailer posing as a retired army officer, and the secret connecting them. Travers has an unusual working arrangement with Scotland Yard, having his own detective agency, but on a consultant basis he's able to call freely upon the services and assistance of Yard personnel.

It's purely a puzzle story, although there's nothing wrong with that, to be sure. The characters do suffer the humility of cavorting with their strings showing, however, and the timetables and alibi-taking could in a word be best described as sloppy. (C)

Charlie's Angels, adapted by Max Franklin from the ABC-TV series (Ballantine 25665; c. 1977; 1st edn, Jan. 1977; 154pp.)

Actually I think perhaps this was the pilot, a made-for-TV movie shown in advance of the series itself. Charlie's client is an heiress to a valuable estate in California wine country, or she will be if she's allowed to return safely to prove her claim. The task of Kelly, Jill and Sabrina is to pave the way, solve a murder, and collect a quarter of a million dollars in the process.

I don't know why anybody would read this. People who watch the show must watch for visual attributes not possibly duplicated in print. People who don't watch know what they are missing.

Max Franklin is a pen-name of mystery writer Richard Deming, and he obviously read the script and watched the show. I don't think he added anything, however, and it all seemed pretty flat to me. Perry Mason never had much background personality either, but he did do his own thinking. What would the angels do without Charlie? (D)

Chelsea Quinn Yarbro, *Ogilvie, Tallant & Moon* (G. P. Putnam's Sons; c. 1976; 214 pp.)

Charles S. Moon is the junior partner of a prosperous San Francisco law firm. Rather than being their token Chinese member, he's their token Indian. (The S. stands for Spotted.) Ofilvie is the political manipulator, Tallant is the society lawyer, and how Charlie got mixed up with these snobs is skipped over pretty lightly.

Malpractice is tough to defend, and since it's a lady doctor involved, it's a case of minority meet minority and compounded when Charlie's new clerk turns out to be Ms. Morgan Studevant, with a huge Male Establishment chip on her shoulder. Everybody's too easily insulted, for my tastes, with plenty of people around to do the insulting, some not so subtly.

Yarbro's a mediocre writer, but she heats the emotional problems up to high intensity. Why do I say mediocre? My rule of thumb is that any writer whose characters pulpishly resort to leering and sneering is doing only half a job. It's a flop as a detective story too, as every reader is going to know at once that the dead drug salesman is connected to the malpractice case. But Charlie has the ancestral gifts of his tribe at his command, and he has to spiritually walk the dead man's last few miles with him before he has the answer. It's a gut-wrenching experience, but for most mystery readers it'll only be a bunch of hooey. (C)

Robert Parker, *Passport to Peril* (Dell 568; c. 1951; 191 pp.)
The front cover is a real eye-grabber. A blonde countess in a black negligee has been tied to a chair and is being threatened with something long and sharp by a short squat man in a black hat. The scene is accurate, but it doesn't reveal too much about the book. I suspect that maybe it says something subtle about the kind of buyer it attracts. The back cover is considerably more informative, featuring as it does a detailed map of Budapest, showing the location of all the action taking place in this Hungarian city freshly under Russian control. At the center of it all is a missing manila envelope, one which will identify the conspirators in a secret neo-Nazi plan to bring on World War III.

Unhappily Robert Parker is not the same fellow who writes about Spenser. This Parker writes like a committee, with each member assigned a chapter and asked to carry on from the point the previous writer left off. It reads as though none of them could be bothered to find out what had happened before, and the characters fall all over themselves trying to keep the plot afloat. Eric Ambler would be an unfortunate choice in comparison, as the ninny in this story seems all too content in his role as unwilling protagonist. With a fractional amount of mental agility he could have just as easily walked the other way when he jumped off the train taking him and his phoney passport further behind the Iron Curtain. (D)

VERDICTS

(More Reviews)

John Dickson Carr, *The Crooked Hinge* (The Mystery Library #2, University Extension UCSD, 1976; orig. pub. 1938; xv + 283pp.; $5.95.)

The second in the Mystery Library's series of reprints is another quality job, and the book itself is a good one. Twenty-five years before the story begins John Farnleigh was packed off to America on the Titanic. He survived and stayed in America, as he was the black sheep of the family, returning only when he inherited the family estate and title. Now, a year later, a man shows up claiming to be the real Sir John Farnleigh. On the night the confrontation takes place to determine the imposter, the first Farnleigh is murdered. Dr. Gideon Fell, somewhat less outrageous here than usual, must determine who killed him (or was it suicide?) and why. There is also a possible tie-in with another murder that happened a year earlier, and a number of Carr's usual strange elements. These include an automaton based on Maelzel's famous Chess Player, a local coven (?), and a truly bizarre solution. An engrossing book.

This edition also contains Dick Conner's indifferent drawings (though the one of Fell is a passable portrait of Chesterton), and an introduction, notes and checklist by Robert E. Briney, that are as fine as his usual work (despite the omission of *To Wake the Dead* from the checklist). (Jeff Meyerson)

John Dickson Carr, *The Crooked Hinge* (introduction, with notes and checklist, by Robert E. Briney, illustrations by Dick Conner. Del Mar: University of California at San Diego University Extension/Publisher's Inc, 1976; originally published in 1938 by Harper and Hamish Hamilton; $5.95.)

The first book in The Mystery Library series was set in a small town in rural Australia. This second Mystery Library book is set ten thousand miles away, in that favorite setting of mystery readers and writers, a small English country house. You may or may not get pleasure out of The Mystery Library books, but you will certainly get variety.

It's 1936, and Sir John Farnleigh is trying to lead the life of a happy country squire. His peaceful existence is shattered when a man calling himself Patrick Gore returns from the past with seemingly conclusive evidence that Farnleigh is not, in fact, Farnleigh. In 1913, "Gore" and "Farnleigh" were both passengers on the *Titanic*. Farnleigh was dabbling in Satanism then, and his father, thinking him a throwback to the Satanist Farnleighs of an earlier day, had him packed off and sent to the States. "Gore" was the child of a circus performer, and spent many years in the circus, having adventures throughout America. Meanwhile, "Farnleigh" was brought up by relatives in Colorado, and only returned to England in 1935, after his older brother, Dudley Farnleigh, died of ptomaine poisoning. "Gore" felt long-suppressed desires to visit his family, and returned to England only to find that Dudley Farnleigh was dead.

"Gore" tries to prove that he is John Farnleigh by answering intimate family details only a Farnleigh would know, standing up under careful questioning by old family servants and Kennet Murray, Farnleigh's childhood tutor. But soon the decisive evidence comes; Farnleigh played with fingerprint kits as a lad, and Murray still has some of the original prints. "Farnleigh" and "Gore" have their fingerprints taken; Murray examines them, and . . . "Farnleigh" is found murdered. It's up to Dr. Gideon Fell (an old friend of Murray's) to solve the murder and decide the knotty problem of the rightful heir.

This is classic detection from the Golden Age--one murder, lots of suspects, lots of clues, and plenty of red herrings. Fell is, of course, the armchair detective *par excellence,* competent, but full of special quirks that set him apart from other series detectives. As a bonus, there is a good deal of supernatural in it, mostly dealing with automata and witchcraft; all the "supernatural" phenomena get explained away in the end, but the occult spell is fun while it lasts--it's pleasantly creepy, but far from frightening. (Carr, by the way, was one of the first writers to lift witchcraft out of the pulps and make it "respectable." As Fritz Leiber puts it, "an aesthetic taste for it was uncommon and when on rare occasions it surfaced fairly well researched in John Dickson Carr's detective stories *The Burning Court* and *The Crooked Hinge,* that was a cause for rejoicing.") The book does suffer from the defect common to many novels of detection where all the characters occasionally run about like chickens with their heads cut off, fussing about the implications of an obscure and quickly forgotten clue. Carr manages to overcome this with a swashbuckling style and the continuing supernatural background. *The Crooked Hinge* is fun, and probably one of the better examples of the classic form. (I did manage to guess who the murderer was, but missed out on the motive.)

A word about the appendices. Dick Conner did the illustrations, and while he may have adjusted his style to suit a belt-press, they are only marginally better than those he did for *The New Shoe,* so I'm happy to see that he didn't illustrate the third TML book. Robert Briney wrote the introduction and notes, and compiled the checklist; the introduction is an appreciation/biography of Carr, and is well done. The notes, though, are only repetitions of the familiar, and could easily be dropped. The checklist is fairly complete, although one Fell book (*To Wake the Dead,* 1937) and the publication date for *The Department of Queer Complaints* (1940) are missing; Briney assures us (in a letter to *TAD*) that these errors will be corrected in future printings, but I wish he could have had enough time to make the checklist a bibliography and given us, say, the first magazine appearances of Carr's short stories, or the original broadcasts of radio shows written by Carr. All in all, Briney's work is competent, but the hype of the TML ads ("appendices, gleaned from obscure and hard-to-find sources, that give fascinating insights into the work and its author") has not yet been fulfilled. (Story A, Extras B) (Martin Morse Wooster)

Newton Thornburg, *Cutter and Bone* (Little, Brown, 1976, 313pp.
    Cutter and Bone cannot, by normal standards, be called
an enjoyable book--it's much too bleak for that. It is an
excellent study of two characters, Rich Bone and Alex Cutter,
trying to get by in a contemporary America as they operate
on the brink of despair. Bone was a successful young execi-
tive in Milwaukee when he suddenly dropped out, leaving his
wife and kids, and drifted across country to Santa Barbara.
His good looks enable him to drift through life, living off
women when he needs money. He has become friends with Cutter, a sardonic, occasionally despairing veteran, who lost a
leg, an arm, and an eye in Vietnam, who lives on his dis-
ability checks and the generosity of a friend. Bone moves
in with him and his common-law wife Mo, who is constantly
stoned; Bone subsequently falls for her. Cutter's is a
savage view of America, and he goes through life lashing out
at everyone and everything, as he searches for some reason
to keep living.
    One night Bone sees a man stuff something in a garbage
can, later discovering that it is a dead body. He thinks
the murderer may have been J. J. Wolfe, a millionaire con-
glomerate head. Cutter sees this as his big opportunity and
sets out to blackmail Wolfe. The mystery element of the
story is present throughout, but the book is mainly the
story of Alex and Rich and the bleakness of the American
dream as they see it as they eat and drink, fight and love,
live and die. They are very real characters who will remain
in your mind long after the final, ironic end. (Jeff Meyerson)

Harry Kemelman, *Wednesday the Rabbi Got Wet* (Morrow, 1976,
219 pp.)
    This is the sixth in Kemelman's acclaimed series about
Rabbi David Small and it is very good indeed, although not
much of a mystery. It is as much about temple politics and
Jewish life in suburban Barnard's Crossing, Massachusetts,
as it is a mystery novel.
    The book's only death (murder is barely even suggested)
involves an old man and his allergy to penicillin, and the
possible switching of two bottles of pills. This is tied in
with the temple matter of the sale of a block of stores and
the purchase of land for a religious retreat, which the rabbi opposes. Suburban Jewish life is limned as sharply as
ever, with some old friends being joined by many new faces.
Though the "mystery" is certainly not great, this is a very
satisfying book. It's as if the people of Barnard's Crossing are old friends: they're still squabbling about temple
directions, still attempting to overrule the rabbi, still
giving in in the end. Warning: read the books in order, as
this gives away the solutions of earlier books. (J. Meyerson)

Harry Patterson, *The Valhalla Exchange* (Stein & Day, 1976,
224 pp.)
    The author of *The Eagle Has Landed* and *Storm Warning*
has once again come up with an exciting thriller set near
the end of World War II--this one literally in the closing
days. As Berlin is being reduced to rubble by the Russian
bombardment, Martin Bormann has a secret plan for escape,
namely to work out an exchange for five important Allied

44

prisoners held in Schloss Arlberg near Innsbruck. He must take over the prisoners before they are turned over to the advancing Allies. Meanwhile the prisoners, led by American general Hamilton Canning, try to convince their guards to surrender. As always Patterson moves effectively from one group to another with skill and ease, building up the page-turning suspense. This one was obviously written with the movies in mind. If it is not quite as good as its two pre-decessors, it is still a well written, fast moving and en-joyable book. (Jeff Meyerson)

Ed McBain, *Even the Wicked* (Signet, 1977, 132 pp.; original-ly published in 1958 as by Richard Marsten.)
Zach Blake and his nine year old daughter Penny return to Martha's Vineyard, where his wife Mary, a championship swimmer, drowned the year before. It seems that Evelyn Cloud, an Indian, sent him a letter saying his wife's death was not an accident. From the moment they reach the island they are warned to leave; when Blake goes to see Evelyn Cloud he finds her murdered, then Penny is kidnapped. What is the secret they are so anxious to keep undiscovered? Does it involve a Nike missile and spies or something more prosaic? The characters aren't particularly involving and the book is unexceptional, but it is a pleasant way to spend an hour or two. (Jeff Meyerson)

Ed McBain, *Death of a Nurse* (Signet, 1976, 160 pp.; orig. pub. 1955 as *Murder in the Navy* by Richard Marsten.)
A nurse is found strangled in the radar room of the U.S.S. Sykes. The list is quickly narrowed down to three suspects, and when one of them apparently commits suicide the FBI is satisfied and closes the case. Lieutenant Chuch Masters of the Navy's investigation board is not satisfied, however, as the drowned man was an expert swimmer. This is, for most of its length, a pretty good book using an unusual setting. Then it is all thrown away on an incredibly bad and stupid ending, using every damsel-in-deadly-peril and will-he-arrive-in-time cliche ever invented, like a bad epi-sode of *The Rookies*. Also, McBain doesn't play entirely fair with the readers, as he withholds important information, then throws it out at the finish. Too bad, as it could have been a much better book. (Jeff Meyerson)

Clive Cussler, *Raise the Titanic!* (Viking, 1977, 314pp, $8.95)
Like its subject matter, *Raise the Titanic!* begins as a sprawling, awesome and majestic adventure novel but ends up sinking in deep water.
An appetizing prelude takes us back in time to the greatest peacetime marine disaster ever--the collision of the luxury liner Titanic with an iceberg in 1912 on her maiden voyage from England to New York. There were not enough life boats for the approximately 2,200 passengers and crew. 1,490 died; 705 survived. An expert blend of facts and fiction makes for a tantalizing prologue.
Now the author takes us to the near future. Working in total secrecy scientists are a step away from completing the ultimate U.S. defense network. To make the system operation-al a rare element called byzanium is needed.

By a strange twist of fate, byzanium was locked in the vaults of the Titanic, now lying twelve thousand feet beneath the surface of the Atlantic Ocean. The President of the United States and a few of his closest advisors mastermind a daring plan--to raise the Titanic.

So far so good. The task of locating the wreck and the technical solutions of lifting it are described in a convincing, absorbing, even breathtaking manner. But then the author shifts gears to an emphasis on cloak-and-dagger intrigue: the Soviet government has gotten hold of the plan, Russian agents infiltrate the salvage operation, an engineer is murdered and a deep-sea submersible is sabotaged.

When the Titanic is brought up to the surface the Russians take advantage of a number of coincidences (a well timed hurricane that must have seemed to them like manna from heaven and the miraculous destruction of all radio contacts), board the ship, threaten the heroic American crew and to prove beyond doubt that they are the Bad Guys humiliate physically the only woman on board.

Then follow four or five melodramatic plot twists in rapid succession, all somewhat cumbersome, too complicated and stretching credibility.

"There is a fascinating aura about the sinking of the Titanic that has gripped thousands of nostalgia freaks, including myself," says the author, Clive Cussler. He is a native Californian who in recent years spent much time diving for lost Spanish galleons, prospecting forgotten gold mines and searching for vanished private aircraft. He has had a long-time interest in researching various mysteries and strange phenomena of the sea, seeing logical explanations for "supernatural" happenings.

His hobby and experiences served him well in providing an ingenious premise with a wealth of meticulous detail. It is unfortunate that the work disintegrated midway into an undisciplined, unharnessed, unbelievable narrative. (Amnon Kabatchnik)

K. Arne Blom, *The Moment of Truth* (Harper & Row, 147 pp., $6.95.)

The quiet, idyllic university town of Lund is hit by unexpected violence.

First there are noisy demonstrations against a distinguished visiting foreign diplomat that mushroom into bloody confrontations with the town's small police force. Then the body of the young and beautiful wife of a police officer is found in her apartment--brutally beaten. There is no apparent motive for her violent death.

Nor for the murder of another young woman. Except that she, too, was a policeman's wife.

Nor for the murder of the next policeman's wife.

The effect of violence on an ordinary, normally peaceful environment is dissected effectively and movingly by a new Scandinavian author. *The Moment of Truth* won the Sherlock Award in Sweden as the best suspense novel of the year.

In parallel tracks the author identifies with the young policemen whose lives are mercilessly shattered and still elicits sympathy for the tortured, demented culprit. With simplicity and tautness he bores into the inner-most sensi-

bilities of the human mind. The procedures of the police
investigation are described in realistic, vivid detail, but
play second fiddle to the tragic human dilemma of ordinary
people fallen victim to the widening cycle of violence in
our age.

K. Arne Blom joins other new voices from Scandinavia,
most notably Maj Sjowall, Per Wahloo and Anders Bodelsen, in
experimenting and adding depth to the somewhat superficial
format of detective fiction. (Amnon Kabatchnik)

Thomas Berger, *Who Is Teddy Villanova?* (Delacorte, 1977);
William Kotzwinkle, *Fata Morgana* (Illus. Joe Servello.
Knopf, 1977).

When mainstream writers invade a genre, the results can
be unpredictable. In this case we have mixed results: one
very good book and one very bad book.

The very bad book first: Thomas Berger is known chiefly
for writing *Little Big Man* which got turned into a great
movie. But Berger is no stranger to crime fiction; early in
the 1960's he wrote a suspenseful book, *Killing Time*.

Who is Teddy Villanova? got the cover on the *New York
Times Book Review* in April 1977 and a lot of nice people are
going to say glowing things about this book.

I am not going to say good things about this book. It
is a silly book; not entertaining-silly like Donald West-
lake's books, but pretentious-silly with Berger's hero
spouting French and German literary quotations to mobsters.
And they answer him back in French and German!

Berger is trying to spoof the hard-boiled detective
novel. He doesn't succeed. He doesn't even succeed in giving the reader a good read. A dull pretentious book: it
must be killed.

Now, to the very good book. If you have any kids, they
probably know Bill Kotzwinkle's work better than you do:
Kotzwinkle's written about a dozen very fine children's
books and a half dozen novels of varying quality. But in
this latest book, superbly illustrated by Joe Servello,
Kotzwinkle has written a great book.

Fata Morgana is a period piece. The time is 1816 and
Paul Picard, Inspector in the Paris Police, is confronted by
an incredible mystery.

The salons of Paris are thrilled by a strange, enigma-
tic couple: the handsome Ric Lazare and his beautiful wife,
Renee. Lazare has a fortune telling machine that can truly
foretell the future. Picard suspects that the man is a char-
latan and is sent over Europe to discover the strange details of Lazare and his wife.

What Picard finds is a wonderful and terrifying story
of magic and murder. Lazare may be as old as five thousand
years. He may be immortal. He has killed in the past, many
times. His wife is variously cast as a whore, a noblewoman,
and may also be immortal.

The book is more than a procedural account of Picard's
investigation. Picard, himself, is a fascinating man, a man
who sees himself as a bloodhound, a preserver of Justice.
The nature of the case, the chase, brings out Picard's character without the moralizing and slowing of plot which results from writers of lesser skills than Kotzwinkle.

The final confrontation, the bloodhound vs. the magician, is very moving, and as thought-provoking an ending as you are likely to read. *Fata Morgana* is a delight. (George Kelley)

Laurie Robeson Wright, *The Perfect Corpse* (Major Books, 1977, $1.50)
This story takes place in a small New England town where nothing ever happens, until one day Bonnie Sturgeon, a school teacher, is found murdered. Her husband George is the obvious suspect but, after he is killed by an explosion in his home, the people in town begin to suspect each other. Grayling Murdoch, school custodian, and friend to everyone, searches for the truth and when he decides he knows who the murderer is, he sets himself out as bait and is almost killed. The story takes many twists and turns and the ending will come as a surprise. An excellent mystery, written with humor, and anyone who has lived in a small town will recognize the authenticity of the town and the people in the book. (Myrtis Broset)

Lesley Egan, *The Blind Search* (Doubleday & Co., 1977)
Attorney Jesse Falkenstein is searching for a nine-year-old girl and her mother, Nonie Johnson, who has removed the child from the home of her foster parents. Each time Falkenstein believed he has traced Nonie he finds it was a mistake. After questioning Nonie's friends and sister with no results, Falkenstein turns to a psychometrist, who gives Jesse a clue he does not recognize until much later. When Nonie Johnson's boyfriend is murdered, it brings in Andrew Clock of the Los Angeles Police Department, who is also Jesse's brother-in-law. Clock attempts to solve his murder case while giving Jesse help with his.
There are glimpses of the family life of the two men which adds a light touch. All Egan fans will want to read this book and those who like to read about police procedure will enjoy it. (Myrtis Broset)

Mark Sadler, *Circle of Fire* (Manor Books, 1977, $1.50)
When Paul Shaw's partner was wounded Shaw goes to investigate. Since his partner was working on a politician's murder, who was killed when his car exploded after he left a roadhouse with a girl, Shaw takes on the case in an effort to try to determine who wanted to kill his partner. Shaw must contend with people who consistently lie to him and begins to wonder if it was the politician who was meant to be murdered, and, if not, who was it and why. The sheriff is friendly and together he and Shaw come up with the solution.
Paul Shaw is reminiscent of Lew Archer. This book is for those who like lots of action in their mysteries. (Myrtis Broset)

Ed McBain, *Ten Plus One* (New American Library, 1977, $1.25)
This is one of the best of the 87th Precinct Mysteries. While detectives Carella and Meyer attempt to find a link between the two prominent men killed by a sniper, a prostitute is shot, then the sniper hits an Italian selling produce at his market, and the detectives must start all over.

Four more people, all from different walks of life, are murdered, one of them as he leaves the precinct. The puzzle--what do all these people have in common. Carella is handed a clue accidentally by the daughter of one of the murdered men but it is not until the sniper attempts to kill another woman that Carella finds the murderer. This is an absorbing mystery. Another plus is the price which is unusual now. (Myrtis Broset)

Michael Innes, *From London Far* (Offset Paperbacks, 1976, $1.95.)

Anyone who buys this book with the thought of other Innes books in mind is due to be disappointed. The story wanders all over the place, the characters are uninteresting, and there is so much excess wordage, it is difficult to tell just what this book is about. Definitely a waste of time to read it. (Myrtis Broset)

Sara Woods, *The Law's Delay* (St. Martin's Press, 1977.)

Anthony Maitland, Barrister, defends Ellen Gray, on trial for the murder of John Wilcox, a friend of Ellen's father, although he believes her to be guilty. It seems clear to Maitland that this murder is connected to one of twenty years ago, when Ellen's father was accused of murdering his wife and her lover. With the help of his friend, Roger Farrell, Maitland delves into the past of Wilcox and his group of friends to find the solution to both murders, despite the hostility of Detective-Inspector Conway of Scotland Yard. Maitland's wife Jenny and his uncle Sir Nicholas Harding are present in their usual roles, familiar to all Maitland fans. Recommended to all mystery readers. (Myrtis Broset)

Carter Brown, *Negative in Blue* (Signet 451-Q6220, 1974, 158 pp.)

I've always had a soft spot in my heart (or is it my head?) for Hollywood-based private eyes. Which is probably why, of the many series characters created by Australian mystery writer Alan G. Yates (who writes as Carter Brown), my favorite is Rick Holman. Holman bills himself as an "industrial consultant," and specializes in clearing up nasty messes, invariably involving homicide, which film colony stars find themselves in, without causing any bad publicity for the stars or studios involved. He, like Shell Scott, is a direct descendant of my beloved Dan Turner, Robert Leslie Bellem's wonderful Hollywood shamus of the pulps, and is one of the very few of the breed still active.

This is the best Carter Brown of recent memory. Two opposing factions are involved in all kinds of skullduggery concerning the negative of an unfinished movie whose female star died from an overdose of barbiturates. A member of one of the factions catches a shotgun blast in the face and Holman steps in to investigate.

Although the process by which Holman solves the mystery is glossed over to the point of being ignored, the pace, as always with Brown, is excellent, building to a stunning, satisfying conclusion. If you haven't yet sampled one of Brown's more than a hundred novesl, here would be a fine place to begin. (Stephen Mertz)

Ian Ousby, *Bloodhounds of Heaven: The Detective in English Fiction from Godwin to Doyle* (Harvard U. Press, $10.00.)

Before detectives could exist in fiction they had to exist in reality, at least in rudimentary form, and once they came into existence their public image and the ways in which fiction writers portrayed them had a reciprocal influence on each other. The process of that interaction in England from the late 18th century to the age of Sherlock Holmes is the subject of this study.

England had no official police during the 1700s, for the forces that operated in Europe at the time were seen as political tools to preserve the power of the ruling class. Instead, the English adopted a kind of primitive free-enterprise law enforcement system, paying bounties to thieves to become thieftakers and turn in their brothers for punishment under the age's brutal criminal laws. Public sympathy for some of the betrayed thieves and outrage at the knowledge that many thieftakers framed innocent people in order to earn more bounty money culminated in the exposure of Jonathan Wild, who was at one and the same time the most successful thieftaker in London and a master thief on a monumental scale. (Holmes in "The Valley of Fear" refers to him as a forerunner of Professor Moriarty.) Anarchist philosopher William Godwin reflected his contemporaries' bitter view of the thieftaker in his *Caleb Williams* (1793), the first English novel with detective overtones.

During the early Victorian era, as the English middle class began to establish itself and as the English police became an official institution of professionals, the translated and heavily fictionalized memoirs of Eugene-Francois Vidocq, chief of the Paris Surete from 1812 to 1827, fostered the image of the detective as an infallible hero larger than life. In real life, however, the English professional police were despised by the public until shortly after the middle of the century. By then the law-and-order morality of the Victorian middle class had combined with internal police reforms and some highly sympathetic portrayals of detectives in journalism and popular fiction to produce a change in public attitude. Inspector Bucket in Dickens' *Bleak House* (1853) and Sergean Cuff in Wilkie Collins' *The Moonstone* (1868) epitomized the detective as a rock of the middle-clsss virtues. And although the police in Conan Doyle's stories at the end of the century are made to look incompetent, they are still solid decent bourgeois, a far cry from the brutal and corrupt thieftakers of a century before, and the image of the unofficial detective as a brilliant if eccentric gentleman and the support of established morality is permanently engrafted onto the literature in the person of Sherlock Holmes.

Such, in a nutshell, is the development Ian Ousby recounts at length in his book, which is exhaustively researched, lucidly written, and a quietly satisfying treat for anyone with an interest in social history, literary history, or in that fascinating genre known as the detective story. (Francis M. Nevins, Jr. Reprinted from the *St. Louis Globe-Democrat*, February 5-6, 1977.)

Myron J. Smith, Jr., *Cloak-and-Dagger Bibliography: An Annotated Guide to Spy Fiction, 1937-1975* (Scarecrow Press, $9.50.)

Devotees of the spy novel or international-intrigue thriller or shoot-em-up are habitually on the alert for authors and titles in the field that are new to them. Until now they had no reference book they could consult in their search for fresh material. The book that now exists, however, leaves them little better off.

Smith's book purports to list and describe some 1,675 works in the genre, arranged by author, with special symbols to designate paperbacks, juveniles, farces, and relatively sexless capers. The best that can be said of the book is that even the most well-versed espionage fan will find some titles here that he hadn't encountered before. However, a fair number of the titles will be new to our spy buff simply because they are not spy stories but main-stream novels, straight war adventures, science-fiction or children's books. And a few will turn out not to exist at all.

The book abounds with errors--of publishers, date, title, series character identification, story description. Thus, of the 45 listed titles by Edward S. Aarons, 14 are accurate, 26 are erroneous on publication dates, and five don't exist. In the entries on Philip Atlee, the Joaquin Hawks series by Bill S. Ballinger, and George Beare, the wrong publisher is given every blessed time. Erskine Childers' *The Riddle of the Sands*, actually published in 1903 and thus far outside the scope of the bibliography, is dated 1940 and described as if it were an anti-Nazi adventure. John Le Carre's *A Murder of Quality*, which is not a spy novel at all but a pure detective story, is included in the compilation, with a hopelessly wrong description. That Mr. Smith knows as little about writing as he does about crime fiction is established by his references to "the daring private eyes of Scotland Yard" and the "briefly-clad girls" of James Bond country.

Despite its abundance of errors, *Cloak-and-Dagger Bibliography* is by no means useless, and most aficionados of the genre will probably be thankful for its availability. But it is unfortunate that a book for which such a need exists doesn't fill that need more completely. (Francis M. Nevins, Jr. Reprinted from the *St. Louis Globe-Democrat*, March 12-13, 1977.)

Larry N. Landrum, Pat Browne and Ray B. Browne, eds., *Dimensions of Detective Fiction* (Popular Press, 1976.)

Scholarly articles on any subject can be deadly dull. This volume of articles on detective fiction is uneven; the articles are grouped into three groups: "The Genre," "Styles" and "The Genre Extended." The best articles are in the "Styles" section.

The articles cover Sherlock Holmes and Nero Wolfe, women mystery writers, Ambler, Mickey Spillane, John D. MacDonald, Chester Himes, Ross Macdonald--and John B. West.

John B. West?

Darwin T. Turner wrote "The Rocky Steele Novels of John B. West" and the credits say it was published in *The Armchair Detective* (August 1973).

I didn't know who John B. West was; I'd seen copies of Rocky Steele Signet paperbacks during my searching in used bookstores. The Rocky Steele books look incredibly tacky; a sample blurb: "Rocky Steele streaks through another fast-paced, fist-throwing round of murder . . . involving a deadly diamond and a blistering babe who is out to nab the rock --and Rocky!"

Yawn.

But Turner's article identifies West as a Black writing about a white private eye modeled on Mickey Spillane's Mike Hammer. Six novels were written between February 1959 and April 1960; shortly afterward, West died.

Turner makes his subject come alive, in sharp contrast to other articles in the volume. Perhaps the fact that the article was written for *TAD* rather than, say, the *Journal for Popular Culture* improves its readibility. Even to the point of forcing me to track down the Rocky Steele books. I'll read them. Someday.

Another interesting, well written article is Raymond Nelson's "Domestic Harlem: The Detective Fiction of Chester Himes." (Reprinted from the *Virginia Quarterly Review*, 48:2.) Again, it forced me to go out and buy the Coffin Ed Johnson and Grave Digger Jones series of six novels. You will be seeing an article on the series from me soon.

The rest are interesting depending on your interest. I found the interview of Ross Macdonald reprinted here was dull. The comparison of Holmes and Wolfe was mercifully short. Others were to incredible to take seriously: " . . . Alienation in Popular Mafia Fiction," and "Sophocles and the Rest of the Boys in the Pulps: Myth and the Detective Novel."

The Turner and Nelson articles are definitely worth your time, the others may interest those of you who'd like to see the academics find deep hidden meanings in Mike Hammer's blasting some mug's stomach out." (George Kelley)

E. Howard Hunt, *Washington Payoff* (1961; originally published as *House Dick* as by Gordon Davis; reprinted 1975 Pinnacle Books), *Where Murder Waits* (1965; originally as by Gordon Davis; reprinted 1973 Fawcett Gold Medal), *Angel Eyes* (1961; as by Robert Dietrich; Dell First Edition), *Return from Vorkuta* (1965; as by David St. John; Signet Books, reprinted 1974).

Watergate lives! Just when we thought we no longer had Nixon to kick around anymore, he surfaces on television. E. Howard Hunt, his mystery writer turned convicted conspirator, has been released from prison and is giving interviews, too.

After his graduation from Brown University and World War II service, Hunt attempted to write full-time, but his books (non-mysteries), though getting good reviews, did not sell well. In 1948 he joined the State Department in a position which served as cover for his C.I.A. activities. He continued to write in order to supplement his income, turning to the fiction of our genre.

Based on the four books I've recently read, I suspect that Hunt's mystery fiction is not memorable. Yet, he may have been better as a writer than he was as a spy, though he is distinctly uneven. As Gordon Davis he is poor. *Washington Payoff* is about hotel detective Pete Novak, an ex-hockey player. When a corpse is discovered at his hotel, he hides the body and proceeds to investigate without bothering to notify the police--the hardboiled equivalent of the sappy Gothic heroine. The extremes in politics, as in cliche-writing, are never that far apart.

Pat Conroy in *Where Murder Waits* is a Washington, D.C., attorney whose mother was Cuban. He fought at the Bay of Pigs and is recruited by anti-Castro forces to locate stolen funds to be used in their efforts to depose the bearded one. In view of his own involvement with the Cuban burglars who were actually caught at the Watergate, Hunt has one very prophetic sentence: ". . . the government can't have a lot of wild-assed Cubans running all over, cutting capers and getting us involved where we oughtn't to be."

The rest of the book consists of such cliches of hard-boiled fiction as: "From above and behind came the soft whistle of something traveling through the air. The instrument caught him precisely above the right ear, pain exploded blindingly, and as he pitched forward . . . ." The plot is confusing, even to the names (Lola and Lilia) of the two girls who find Conroy irresistible. Incidentally, girls always find Hunt's heroes irresistible.

As Robert Dietrich, Hunt wrote nine paperback originals regarding Washington, D.C., C.P.A. Steve Bentley. Since, unlike any other accountant I've met, Bentley is constantly involved in intrigue and murder, I wonder if Hunt wasn't enjoying a small joke with the C.P.A.-C.I.A. similarity. As Dietrich, Hunt plotted a bit more carefully and wrote some good action scenes. *Angel Eyes* concludes with a genuinely exciting scene near the Jefferson Memorial. It, too, is prophetic in its subject matter: tapes which can destroy a Washington political figure. At one point we have Bentley saying, "Don't think I can't smell a cover-up in the making." In 1961 yet!

Peter Ward, hero of the spy stories Hunt wrote as David St. John, shares many characteristics with Hunt. He is a graduate of Brown (an ex-hockey player) and has a cover for his C.I.A. activities, a Washington, D.C., law practice. His wife was killed while with him on a C.I.A. assignment. Ironically, while Hunt languished in prison, following his arrest, his own wife was killed in a plane crash while raising funds for his defense.

Of the St. John series, *Return from Vorkuta* is the best I've read. It's written with a certain amount of sophistication, and its background of Spanish history and the monarchy is unusual. A later book in the series, *The Venus Probe* (1966), is almost embarrassing in its pro-C.I.A. attitude, picturing their agents as over-worked and under-paid.

Reports have circulated that Howard Hunt, under his own now-famous name, is writing a book about his experiences in the last five years. Another selection for the Watergate Book Club! (Marvin Lachman)

Bill S. Ballinger, *Heist Me Higher* (Signet, 1969, 125 pp.)
Heist Me Higher starts out well enough, with Bryce Patch witnessing a payroll robbery at Neo-Electronics Corporation and setting out to find the crooks (he is the head of the Amsterdam Investigation Bureau). But the story

starts to go downhill fast when Leda Claysmith arrives to
persuade Bryce to find her ex-husband. Soon every woman
B. P. meets is dragging him off to bed. Ballinger obviously
meant this to be humorous, but it kills all interest in the
mystery. Even the dialogue deteriorates: "I'm itching for a
chance to heat you up--all of you! Right in the guts!"
When another couple of people are murdered, Patch quickly
finds the answers and wraps up the case, but by then the
only reaction is . . . who cares? Skip it. (Jeff Meyerson)

Donald Hamilton, *The Removers* (Fawcett, 1961, 176 pp.)
     Matt Helm gets a letter from his ex-wife asking for his
help, but when he arrives at her ranch he discovers her new
husband is Larry "the Duke" Logan, a tough Englishman who
can take care of himself. This ties in with Helm's assignment: to find out why a top Russian agent is working for
gangster Sal Fredericks as a bodyguard, where it turns out
the Duke was his predecessor. Matt gets involved with Fredericks' daughter Moira and her dog Sheik (a memorable character) on the way to a final bloody confrontation and the
ultimate solution. The writing is fine, as usual, and Matt
Helm is an effective and curiously sympathetic character.
(Jeff Meyerson)

Anthony Armstrong, *The Trail of Fear* (Macrae-Smith, 1927;
Methuen, 1931.)
     London is plagued by a dope ring, and the astute Detec-
tive-Inspector Harrison of Scotland Yard is one of the men
on its trail. He discovers a pusher and follows him. A
rendezvous with a supplier takes place, and Harrison bides
his time until he spots the supplier making contact with a
higher up. Harrison immediately arrests the latter and
finds evidence on his person.
     Cut to Jimmie Rezaire, the head of the dope ring, who
has several disguises and hiding places to mask his illegal
activities. He notices a suspicious-looking watcher outside
his premises, and realizes that the game is nearly up. His
plans are made. A car in a nearby garage will take him to
Beaulieu where a motor launch waits to take him to the Chan-
nel Islands and, eventually, France where safety and the
proceeds of his crimes await.
     Rezaire foolishly bides his time. Enter three members
of the drug ring. This extra group will seriously compli-
cate his plans for escape. Then the police make their move.
     There follows the longest (270 pages), most sustained
chase that I can recall in a thriller.
     Rezaire, the protagonist, is obviously an early example
of the anti-hero due to his profession, but his plight and
desperate efforts to escape do manage to arouse sympathy in
the reader. He is very clever, and the obverse of the much
more admirable Father Brown. He can often put himself into
the minds of the police and determine what their next move
against him will be. Rezaire is a resourceful rogue, and
his 24 hour race to destiny is quite an experience.
     The Trail of Fear is fast, furious, suspenseful, often
ingenious, and full of action and physical movement. It
bears comparison with the work of such specialists in this
genre as Geoffrey Household and Alfred Hitchcock. (C. Shibuk)

Erle Stanley Gardner, *The Case of the Troubled Trustee* (Morrow, 1965.)

Here's another routine Perry Mason from Gardner's last years, as fast-paced as ever but incredibly amateurish in construction and execution. Mason's client is a young investment counselor who has violated several fiduciary duties in order to protect the lovely trust beneficiary from a bearded leftist beatnik equipped with a gargoyle mother and a scheme to use the trust corpus to subsidize other beatniks. a proxy fight over oil stock that should have been but isn't in the trust portfolio leads to murder and an unusually long trial sequence, highlighted by Hamilton Burger's savage cross-examination of Mason's client. Mason's trap to catch the real killer is as nutty as the so-called reasoning that led him to devise it, and he never bothers to explain how the murderer came by the knowledge needed to carry out the frame-up. All in all, an uneven and unappetizing specimen of ESG's sad last decade. (Francis M. Nevins, Jr.)

Erle Stanley Gardner, *The Case of the Beautiful Beggar* (Morrow, 1965.)

A young woman who claims to be the niece of a wealthy 75-year-old businessman begs Perry Mason to rescue her uncle from some greedy relatives who have had the old man declared incompetent, put him into a mental institution, and gotten themselves appointed conservators of his property. Mason's handling of the civil proceedings as to the old gentleman's sanity and his gorgeous banking gimmick to get some of his client's money back occupy the first half of the book. Late in the game comes the inevitable murder-and-trial complex, but the criminal side of this case is extremely perfunctory and dull, and punctuated by incredible runs of lucky guesswork on Mason's part. Gardner, who was himself 75 when he wrote the story, seems to have been all too vividly aware of how easily unscrupulous relatives with a hired doctor and lawyer in their pockets can railroad a mentally sound old person into a death-trap sanitarium. This novel is both the most excitingly inventive and the most deeply personal of all the late Mason adventures. (Francis M. Nevins, Jr.)

Erle Stanley Gardner, *The Case of the Worried Waitress* (Morrow, 1966.)

This one opens tantalizingly as the client of the title asks Mason to find out why her aunt is pretending to be broke and yet hiding a fortune in her hatboxes. Soon the waitress is charged first with robbing and later with near-fatally assaulting her aunt, and in trying to clear her Mason becomes involved in a battle between rival wives over their late husband's estate and between rival power blocs over control of a corporation, with an elusive blind woman apparently up to her neck in both conflicts. But despite the fascinating story elements. the book's organization and execution are ghastly. Gardner makes not the least attempt to explain what really happened in several key sequences, and at the flat and boring trial Hamilton Burger literally forgets to present evidence that a crime was even committed! If ever a book was written while the author was asleep, this is it. (Francis M. Nevins, Jr.)

THE DOCUMENTS IN THE CASE

(LETTERS)

From Jeff Banks, P.O. Box 3007 SFA Sta., Nacogdoches, TX:
Pardon this being handwrit, please. You won't hurt my feelings if you don't publish it. I've made my feelings plain
on letters of comment elsewhere--I think they're a waste of
space--and I've had several l.o.c.'s published with that
opinion in them stated in various ways. I write to you, not
to the general readership. /// Anyway a letter is all you
get from me this month. And what with finals at the college where I teach and a couple of bona fide medical crises
in the family, it was a matter of sweating a deal of blood
to find the time even for this. /// Best item in this issue
was Dick Thorpe's lovely, nostalgic look at the pulps. I'm
a pulp fan from further back than I like to remember, and
naturally the older we get the more nostalgic we become.
Also, I enjoy checklists, tho I find it hard to believe that
Art or anyone else can enjoy typing them. . . . (What do
you do about longhand elipses?) /// Your decision on the
Wolfe saga suits me fine. This first installment was ex-
cusably long, but perhaps you'll be able to put the others
on a diet to keep them from being quite so stout . . . . ///
Steve's review column was welcome as always. I'm delighted
we agreed on *The Man with Bogart's Face*. Just like always,
I disagree with him on a couple of other books he mentions
and agree on still others. Finally, and most of all, I
thank him for calling my attention to M. Douglas's *The Deadly Games*. It's now on my Must Read list. /// Likewise, I
appreciate the Mike Nevins review of *Buyer Beware* by Lutz.
PI yarns are my favorite reading (excepting those over-pub-
licized Archers), and I'm always delighted to find out about
one I didn't know existed. /// I've a question regarding
the *Gator* review: what is "thich grass," a special Florida
swamp variety, perhaps the "poison grass" of the *Alligator*
review?--or did I catch you in a typo? /// While on the
subject of reviews, let me hark briefly back to mine in the
previous issue, I'd expected a legion of feminists to casti-
gate me in your letter column. But no controversy arose.
Does the HEW know you have no feminist readers? Also, the
final comment I made, regarding Ted Mark, was a sly way of
checking if you had any more TM fans (besides myself) among
your readers. As usual, the sage of the girlie mags was the
first in the field. His fine non-series novel *Regina Blue*
(Dell, 1972) had a liberated professional woman as its heroine. It is also a passable locked room murder, satirizes
Agatha Christie (and a host of other targets) and is packed
with the kinky humor that made Ted Mark the toast of the
Sixties. Care for a retrospective review? I'll review my
favorite "tec" magazine, a 1950's *Manhunt*, in time for publication in your fifth issue.
[*Of course "thich grass" is a specific kind of poison grass.
I thought everybody knew that. Me make a typo? How could
you even mention such a think? /// By all means, lay on
with the retrospective review, and I'll take your remarks
re* Manhunt *as a commitment. (You heard him, folks.) /// I*

56

*don't know how many feminist readers TMF has, but female sub-
scribers are outnumbered by males by about four to one. I
wonder what that means.]*

From George Kelley, 505 N. Carroll St. #503, Madison, WI:
I was very happy to see your Stout Saga. Please don't get
down on yourself about breaking your pledge. I've been
about to read all the Stout books in order myself, and this
gives me a great opportunity to read along with your Saga.
/// Keep the checklists coming. I find them very helpful
and useful. /// Lastly, I'd like to make a suggestion:
could you organize the reviews into "New books (paper & hard-
cover)" and "Retrospective Reviews"? This would be an enor-
mous help. I like to read reviews of recent books first,
especially paperbacks so I can buy them before they disap-
pear from the stands or go out-of-print. One more suggestion (you're going to hate this one): could *TMF* list a yearly index of books reviewed? This would aid in finding reviews without going through all the issues. The biblio-
philes among us would love you for such a feature.
*[Okay. Your badgering, and that of others, has finally led
me to separate reviews of new books from those of old ones.
Effective this issue all reviews of new material (or newly
re-issued material) will appear at the front of each review
section, and retrospective reviews will take up the rear.
There is no special division, but when you get to the first
oldie all the rest will be oldies too. Unless I screw up
and get one or two out of place. Does this suit? /// I
like the idea of a yearly index of books reviewed, but I'd
like for someone else to do all the work on it if possible.
Any takers?]*

From Martin Morse Wooster, Box 1691 Beloit College, Beloit,
WI 53511:
Shibuk's review of *The Girl's Head* was quite interesting,
by the way. Was the 1937 edition a revision, an update, or
just a reprint? It would seem quite hard to transform a
tale of Tsarist intrigue into a novel of Stalinist excesses.
/// I wish you hadn't printed the review of *Beak!* It's
probably your review, because it followed the Kabatchnik reviews, and seemed to be a commentary on them. But Kabatchnik reviewed suspense novels, you were reviewing sf. Mind
you, I'm a sf/mystery fan, but I like my sf separated from
my mystery reading. You should have saved the *Beak!* review
for DAPA-EM. (Now if Kabatchnik had reviewed books about
giant mutant killer crocks . . . .) /// Keep getting Stu
Shiffman to do more work for you. His spot illos were excellent, and his cover pretty good. Now if you could get
Frank Miller to do a cover . . . . /// Enclosed is a review
of *The Crooked Hinge.* You will note that I am now giving
two grades for Mystery Library books—one for the story itself, and one for the appendices. Appendices will be judged
on the quantity of original material contained therein, and
whether the information contained in them is useful, novel,
and complete. *The New Shoe*'s grades would have been B for
the story and C+ for the extras.

From Charles Shibuk, 2084 Bronx Park E., Bronx, NY 10462:

In regard to one of the suggestions offered by Mr. Banks: If
a checklist of mystery films denotes insanity on the compil-
er's part, I'm afraid that I must plead guilty. /// Many
years ago, when we were both younger and stronger, Marv Lachman and I produced a lengthy and exhaustive series entitled
"Dramatizations of the Great Literary Detectives and Crimi-
nals" for *TAD*. /// This series included radio (C. S.--Vol.
1, No.2), television (M. L.--Vol. 1, No. 3), and theater (M.
L.--Vol. 1, No. 4). /// My film material appeared in Vol. 2,
Nos. 1 and 3. /// I specified author, name of series character, actor(s) who impersonated him/her, names of film(s),
literary source (if necessary), date, and country of origin
--if not produced in America. Shorts, serials, and screen
originals not based on previously published material were
identified as such. /// This particular series was cited by
Barzun and Taylor in *A Catalogue of Crime* on p. 613. /// A
further instance of instability on my part was the addenda
to "*Who Done It?*: The Mystery Novel on the Screen" which appeared in Vol. 3, No. 4 of *TAD*. /// 4 pages were devoted to
correcting Mr. Hagen's errors. Some 11½ pages listed omissions. All material which had appeared in the previous
"Dramatizations" series was ignored to prevent duplication
for *TAD* readers. /// The format listed author, country of
origin, date, film title, original source--if necessary, and
leading player. /// Letters by knowledgeable readers and
myself indicated corrections and numerous additions to both
lists. /// Much of the former material and some of the latter was incorporated into *Encyclopedia of Mystery and Detection*. /// Those were really the good old days of *TAD*.
[*Lest there be any confusion, I hasten to say that it was I,
not Jeff, who suggested that anyone who would tackle such a
task must be crazy.*]

Mike Nevins, 4466 W. Pine Blvd., #23-C, St. Louis, MO 63108:
It will be a few weeks before I'll be able to send you some
more reviews for your next issue, but I wanted to let you
know that I think *TMF* #3 is your best and meatiest issue yet.
/// I was pleased to see Nick Carr's tribute to his distinguished relative. Late this year *TAD* will be running my
article on JDC's radio plays, including dates, descriptions,
discussions, and a letter Carr wrote me on the subject of
radio back in 1975. It was in 1942, not '43, by the way,
that Carr began work on *Suspense*. And as for Carr stories
in the pulps, his cousin as well as all other pulp collec-
tors will be delighted to learn that there is at least one
uncollected original Carr story buried in an obscure old issue: "Terror's Dark Tower," in *Detective Tales*, 10/35. Carr
later recycled the gimmick in this story, but the original
version has a grand guignol flavor all its own, plus a de-
tective--Sir James Fenwick, former head of the Indian Secret
Police--who appears nowhere else in Carr's works. (The pulp
soty mentioned by Nick Carr, "The Burning Court," is of
course merely a condensation of Carr's classic 1937 novel.)
/// It was good to see your Nero Wolfe series in print
again and moving forward. For my money your account is a
vast improvement on the Baring-Gould book. /// Funny how
different readers react differently to the same book. Contrary to Jeff Meyerson, I thought *Nightmare in Pink* was one

of the best McGees, but didn't care at all for *The Quick Red Fox* which Jeff probably thinks the high point of the whole series . . . .

From Jeff Meyerson, 50 1st Place, Brooklyn, NY 11231:
Thanks for another fine issue of *TMF*, and thanks to all those who supplied the fifth Clinton-Baddeley title--maybe I will pick it up in London this summer (yes, we're going again). Bob Briney's emendations to the Crossen checklist were extremely useful--the two combined make a pretty complete list. /// I'm glad you decided to run the entire Saga in *TMF*; rereading it shows what a fine achievement it is. My first experiences with Stout were unmemorable--*Where There's a Will*, *Fer-de-Lance* and *Death of a Dude*--but I've since read two of his best efforts--*Too Many Cooks* and *A Family Affair*. I'll eventually read them all. /// I enjoyed the Thorp and Carr articles and the Popular Library checklist; it's interesting how 1-76 were mysteries, but non-mysteries came to take over more and more of their list. Either Steve is mellowing or he's been reading better books lately--all but four of his books were As and Bs! /// After reading the reptile reviews, your *Beak!* (wasn't it yours?) doesn't sound that far-fetched. *Croc'* sounds the best to me. /// I can understand John Ball's anger at Martin Wooster's review, but it doesn't change the fact that Dick Conner's illustrations for *The Crooked Hinges* are not good either, in my opinion. I did enjoy *The Mystery Story*, despite some repetition. I don't think the letter section is too long--on the contrary, it is one of the best sections of *FANcier*, with interesting information, opinions and suggestions. I'd hate to see it cut. Jeff Banks' Mystery Movie idea is a good one. Also needed are production company and original source (novel, play, etc.). I don't think the producer is necessary. I really don't have the time to take on such a monumental project at present, but I'd be willing to contribute to anyone who does. (If no one volunteers I might reconsider, but it doesn't look promising.) /// I finally received a response from Avon about the Classic Crime Collection. It wasn't any help on titles, but did give me some information on how the books were chosen and why the series was dropped. I have what I think is a complete checklist--as soon as I can get a few missing book numbers and publication dates I'll do a short article. If anyone has the following information, please send it to me to complete the article: *The Expendable Man* (date-9/69?), *Death of a Doll* (date-11/69?), *The Room Upstairs* (date-1/70?), *The Chinese Bell Murders* (date-3/70?), *Maigret and the Headless Corpse* (# and date), *Whatever Happened to Baby Jane?* (# and date).

From Marv Lachman, 3410 B Paul Ave., Bronx, NY 10468:
Regarding the March issue (albeit belatedly): 1. After several re-readings I think I like Rik Thompson's continuation of "The *EQMM* Cover Murders." If I'm attaching the right name to the right face, I believe I've met Mr. Thompson at each of the last four Bouchercons. If so, I hope to get the chance to talk to him in person about the story this fall when Bouchercon should be in New York. 2. I enjoyed most of the reviews you published, although some of them give away

too many of the surprises to be found (one hopes) within the
books reviewed. I've got a theory that reviews of mysteries
should tell practically nothing of the plot and should, in
addition to telling what kind of mystery it is (e.g. spy,
suspense, classic deduction etc.), only put it in historical
perspective, and then, tell whether the reviewer liked it.
After enough reviews, the reader can determine if his tastes
and those of the reviewer coincide. If so, he can look for
the books his favorite reviewer recommends. Do the readers
of *The Mystery FANcier* share my feelings? 3. I hope to see
more articles like those on Crossen and Pronzini. I also
liked the Dell Map checklist though it came too late to do
me much good. As a collector of these examples of the "Gold-
en Age of Paperbacks" myself, I had compiled my own list the
hard way. 4. I'm glad you have nothing against paranoia and
printed Mike Avallone's ravings in the March issue. The article could have been fun if you had not deleted the names.
I doubt if anything Mr. Avallone said was libelous. "Death
of a .300 Hitter"???? I'm afraid Mr. Avallone's batting average is nowhere that high. As a baseball fan I hope he'll
forgive me if I say it's more like Al Brancato of the 1940
Philadelphia A's. However, I'd like to recommend the baseball story Mr. Avallone did for the 12/64 issue of *EQMM*.
It's called "Take Me Out to the Ball Game," and it has one
of the best closing lines I've ever read. /// The four co-
authors and co-editors (of whom I'm one) of *The Encyclopedia
of Mystery and Detection* have been nominated for MWA Edgars.
The awards dinner is on April 29, so until then I'm walking
around with my fingers crossed; it's not easy to type that
way. [LATER] I very much enjoyed your May issue, especially the piece on Carr and Dickson Thorpe's enthusiastic piece
on the old pulps. I love reading about the old magazines
and dearly regret not having saved the pulps I had when I
was a kid in the early 1940's. However, I retain enough
sanity not to start collecting now; I have enough collecting
addictions without *that* one. /// I hope your problems regarding having enough material are soon solved. If everyone
who writes a letter saying, "Why doesn't someone write an
article about so-and-so?" would sit down and write it himself, you'd have no problems I suspect. I'm very favorable
to your doing the Nero Wolfe series, having just finished
all of Stout's books myself. Whatever minuses there were in
these books were more than offset by some of the unique pluses Stout offered us. I suspect I'll have more comments as
the series progresses. /// I'm just recuperating from one
of the real thrills of a lifetime. I and my co-conspirators
received "Edgars" for *The Encyclopedia of Mystery and Detection* at the annual MWA awards dinner. Suddenly, a lot of
work was all worth while. [. . .] Are you interested in a
list of the first 500 titles from Pocket Books. I believe I
have the entire list, though about 300 are non-Mysteries.
Let me know.
[*Congratulations to you and your cohorts, Marv, for the well-
deserved Edgar. /// Am I interested in a list of the first
500 Pocket Books? (Groan.) I hate typing those bloody
lists, but if TMF's readership wants it I'll martyr myself.
(How about it, folks?) Or maybe I can talk Art Scott into
typing it for me. He likes typing lists, remember?*]

From Edmund S. Meltzer, 321 Bloor Street West, Toronto, Ontario M5S 1S5, Canada:

I have just discovered your delightful journal, and I have read with much interest and appreciation the first installment of your series on "The Nero Wolfe Saga" (*TMF* 1 #3, May); I look forward to its sequels. The chronological arrangement, with the focus on the development of the characters and other elements of the saga from one story to the next, is extremely illuminating. As you observe, these aspects do not emerge as clearly in Baring-Gould's book; he seems more intent on harmonizing the corpus into a consistent whole, and thus inconsistencies tend to be smoothed over. /// A few footnotes on matters of detail have occurred to me in the course of reading your article. Wolfe's "relapses" are not first described in *The Red Box*, but at the outset in *Fer-de-Lance* (pp. 53 ff. of the Pyramid paperback edition), where we are also treated to a description of Wolfe "in deshabille" (p. 45). Another trait of Archie's in the first book which is fortunately absent later on is a somewhat sycophantic fulsome tone which he occasionally adopts in speaking of Wolfe's genius. Regarding the title *Some Buried Caesar*, while it is a direct quotation from Fitz-Gerald's rendition of the *Rubaiyat*, it cannot help recalling to the majority of readers Antony's better-known line from Shakespeare's *Julius Caesar*, "I come to bury Caesar, not to praise him." Indeed, I wonder whether FitzGerald himself was influenced by this Shakespearean line when he translated the passage, as the original Persian says nothing about "Caesar", but simply. "Every place where there have been a rose and a tulip-bed,/ it has come from the redness of some prince's blood" (A. J. Arberry, *The Romance of the Rubaiyat*, London, 1959, p. 204). Moreover, "Caesar" is not yet present in FitzGerald's first attempt (in Latin) to translate the *Rubaiyat* (*Ibid*., p. 63). /// When Wolfe says "where you're at," is he necessarily making a grammatical error? Had this expression, with its distinct idiomatic import different from "where you are," penetrated beyond dialectal use by 1946? (In any case, I must agree that it would be out of character for Wolfe.) And also, permit me to come to the defense of the lovely ladies you disparage as "those 'Southern Belle' phonies." Perhaps in your case familiarity has bred contempt, but I must confess to being charmed by the couple of Southern Belles I am fortunate enough to know, and by their speech. (It would be distinctly unchivalrous to say more.) Regarding "chitlins", perhaps we should bear in mind that the spelling is Archie's (*cf.* "noovoh reesh" in *Fer-de-Lance*, where however his tongue is in his cheek); had Wolfe himself been recording the case, he doubtless would have used the preferable "chitterlings".

[*Thanks for the several corrections; I hope other readers will be similarly helpful in pointing out errors and omissions in the series, so that I can make it as complete and accurate as possible when I redo it. As to whether Wolfe's "where you're at" constitutes a grammatical error, I am not the person to say (though I did), since the rules of English grammar have always been a mystery to me and I always play it by ear, but at the very least the "at" is superfluous. As for the chitterlings/chitlins comment,* (Continued on p. 2)

www.ingramcontent.com/pod-product-compliance
Lightning Source LLC
Chambersburg PA
CBHW021223020426
42331CB00003B/441